A PRACTICAL GUIDE

TO LANGUAGE

LEARNING

A PRACTICAL GUIDE

TO LANGUAGE

LEARNING

A Fifteen-Week Program of Strategies for Success

H. Douglas Brown
San Francisco State University

1989

McGraw-Hill Publishing Company

New York St. Louis San Francisco Auckland Bogotá Caracas
Hamburg Lisbon London Madrid Mexico Milan
Montreal New Delhi Oklahoma City Paris San Juan
São Paulo Singapore Sydney Tokyo Toronto

This is an EBI *book*

A Practical Guide To Language Learning:
A Fifteen-Week Program of Strategies for Success

1 2 3 4 5 6 7 8 9 0 MAL MAL 8 9 4 3 2 1 0 9

ISBN: 0-07-008208-1

CONTENTS

1   Can I Learn a Foreign Language?   1

You can be successful in your foreign language learning venture by taking charge of your own learning and by finding your own pathways to success. Don't leave everything up to your instructor and textbook.

Exercises for Week One

2   Set Your Own Goals.   5

There are many practical contexts in today's world in which you can use your knowledge of a foreign language. By developing and setting your own personal goals for learning, you increase your chances of success.

Exercises for Week Two

3   Born to Win.   9

As you may get overwhelmed with the task of learning a complex set of skills, self-confidence is important. Your overall global self-confidence can help you to overcome feelings of self-doubt.

Exercises for Week Three

4   Don't Worry!   13

Foreign language anxiety, like math anxiety, comes from a fear of failing, of falling flat on your face, of looking like a fool. That fear can be overcome through cooperative learning and positive thinking.

Exercises for Week Four

5   Take the Plunge!   17

As you get rid of the fear, you have to be willing to take risks, to plunge in even though you may be wrong. By learning how to take calculated risks, you can move forward in your new language with confidence.

Exercises for Week Five

HOW TO USE THIS GUIDE

The goal of *A Practical Guide to Language Learning* is to provide beginning foreign language students with a general guide to the language learning process. Although the *Guide* is part of the ancillary package provided to instructors who have adopted an introductory Random House foreign language textbook, it was prepared with your students in mind. There are two easy ways for you to make this material available to your students if you would like them to have it.

You are free to have all the material in this book photocopied for each of your students who are using a Random House introductory language textbook. The book has been produced in a format that lends itself to photocopying, and Random House grants you the right to have it photocopied and distributed to your students as part of the package that accompanies its first-year language books.

If you would prefer to have some or all of your students purchase the book, at a very low cost, your bookstore manager can place an order with the Random House College Division/McGraw-Hill, Inc. for the appropriate number of copies.

PREFACE

It is sometimes assumed that in-class activities, a textbook, and some homework exercises are sufficient for successful learning of a foreign language. In the classroom, students work with an instructor and interact with one another, follow a textbook faithfully, and then go home to read and practice a variety of material. Is that enough? According to a growing number of new research studies, it isn't. These studies have found that successful learners spend a significant amount of time outside of the classroom doing such things as setting personal goals, seeking out opportunities for practice, systematically analyzing their errors, and developing a number of little gimmicks, techniques, and games—in short, finding their own pathways to success.

This book capsulizes these research findings and converts them into practical exercises for learners. In lighthearted, understandable terms, each chapter succinctly highlights a major factor that learners need to pay attention to. The exercises at the end of the chapter help students to create opportunities for learning both within and beyond the classroom. Included among the exercises are guidelines on how the technique of writing a diary or journal can aide in the quest for success.

The book is designed to accompany an introductory course in a foreign language. Its fifteen brief chapters form a semester-long program of strategies for successful learning. Just a few minutes of reading on a weekly basis will inform learners and provide specific individual and small-group activities for the week that will enrich the process of learning.

This book makes a variety of research on the psychology of language learning accessible for the first time to foreign language learners themselves. The research reflected here is comprehensive and current. Several dozen practical exercises are directly available to learners. The information and activities apply to the learning of any foreign language. At the same time, no outlandish promises are made—in fact, readers are warned that they should beware of those who come to them promising instant, painless, effortless success.

To the student The ultimate message here is that you can *do* something to take charge of your own destiny in your journey toward success. Remember, this book is not a replacement for your classroom work. Rather, it is a supplement to those valuable in-class activities that should help you to make better use of time spent inside and outside of the classroom. If you're faithful to the weekly exercises and to getting the most out of a bit of diary writing, you should be able to find your own unique pathway to success.

To the instructor If the students in your classes will follow this book with just a modicum of faithfulness, you should find your classroom enriched by a more enthusiastic and inquisitive group of students. Encourage them to use the book! It need not take any of your classroom time at all since it is intended for individual use outside of the classroom. It is designed to complement virtually any teaching method, yet you may find that you will want to tailor some of your lessons to incorporate selected strategies that your students are working on. Perhaps, too, by sharing with your students your own experiences in foreign language learning—the frustrations, embarrassing moments, joys, and victories— you can create an atmosphere of cooperative learning in which everyone wins.

In my own journey as a teacher, I'm especially grateful to all those students whose ingenuity allowed them to create numerous personal strategies, from the bizarre to the ridiculous. I want to thank them for sharing their formulas and partial formulas for success. Special thanks go to language learners Susan Checkley and Lynn Perkins for their assistance in the preparation of this manuscript.

H. Douglas Brown

CHAPTER ONE

Can I Learn a Foreign Language?

You are about to take a journey. The journey will take you through sounds and sentences, across paragraphs and poems, and into new vistas of experience. As you enter your foreign language and it becomes a part of you, a new world of people and places and ways of thinking will open up to you.

Your journey will be an exciting one, but it's going to take a lot of work and effort. At times you may have some self-doubt: Can I really learn a foreign language—I mean, learn to *use* this language fluently for something besides passing exams or getting through the foreign language requirement? Do I have a knack for languages? Am I too old? (Little kids seem to do better at languages.) Is language learning really something that I'm cut out to do?

Questions like these are addressed in this book. It's a book that will help you to be all that you can be in a foreign language. It will give you some creative ideas on how to become a successful language learner. It will give you some hints on developing your very own, personal pathways to achieving your goals. It will help you get over some of the blocks that prevent people from being successful. This book will show you how important it is for you to think positively. It will persuade you to take charge of your *own* learning, and not leave everything up to a textbook or a teacher.

You see, there is plenty of research now that shows that almost anyone can learn a foreign language by creating a positive, optimistic learning environment and following certain strategies for success. There are lots of very ordinary people who have become fluent in foreign languages by following some basic principles.

Sometimes people fail to learn a foreign language simply because they don't know *how to learn* a foreign language. They walk into the classroom and expect to study a language as they would study history or economics. Well, you can't do that with a language. Learning a language requires a complex set of skills that involves your whole self—your emotional self, thinking self, and physical self. It's a skill that involves a special blend of positive attitude, concentration, effort, and relaxation.

At the same time, there's no quick-fix program anywhere that will make this journey an easy one. You may have seen some of those magazine advertisements that promise you the world if you'll just listen to some cassettes. They want you to think that their product will give you success painlessly. Well, beware! You've got to be willing to put in your fair share of effort, and that effort amounts to a lot more than just sitting back and listening to some tapes. If you dive into this language with a willingness to try hard, and with a belief that you can actually do it, then you will be successful!

So don't say you're too old, or you don't have the knack, or you're afraid to look like a fool, or you'll just do enough to get by. You *can* learn this foreign language and learn enough to *do* something with it! This book puts some of the very latest knowledge in the field at your disposal, and that knowledge is your ticket to an exciting journey.

In case you think this book is going to do everything for you, keep in mind a couple of things it does not do. It doesn't go into any detail on the bits and pieces of your particular language (sounds, words, roots, endings, tenses, gender, etc.). Those things are so specific to your foreign language that you should rely on your teacher, your textbook, and your intuition to figure out how to tackle them.

Also, this book does not give you explanations on how the research was conducted that finally led to the principles that are passed on to you here. For more complete information on this fascinating process of foreign language learning, you might want to read another book that I've written: *Break the Language Barrier: Finding Your Pathways to Success*, by H. Douglas Brown (Intercultural Press, 1989). And if you want highly technical information on both learning and teaching a foreign language, then read *Principles of Language Learning and Teaching* (Second Edition), by H. Douglas Brown (Prentice-Hall, Inc., 1987).

What this book does for you is this:

1. It sets a general "tone" with which you can approach the language you're learning.

2. It describes how successful language learners are able to develop effective combinations of emotional, intellectual, and physical abilities.

3. It helps you to believe in yourself and to take charge of your own learning above and beyond your classroom activities.

4. It helps you to understand yourself as a language learner and to discover your own unique strategies for success.

5. It gives you helpful ideas for working cooperatively with your teacher and with your classmates, all of whom are members of a team.

At the end of each of the fifteen chapters of this book, you'll find exercises. These are provided for you to do on a weekly basis as you take your journey. The exercises, a product of research and of the experiences of successful language learners, are designed to help pave the way to the accomplishment of your own goals. The fifteen sets of exercises in each chapter are intended to take you through a typical fifteen-week semester. If your course is shorter or longer, adjust the exercises to suit yourself.

Exercise for Week One

For this week, there's just one basic exercise that will help you gain some valuable insights into your own learning process. It's one that has worked remarkably well for many language learners: keeping a journal (a diary of your personal feelings, thoughts, ideas, fears, successes, problems, frustrations, breakthroughs) of your ongoing experience in learning this language.

You may never have kept a diary or journal before. That's okay. Now is a perfect time to start. Just find a sturdy notebook with plenty of blank pages in it and start writing. Your journal should be completely spontaneous. Any thought that comes into your head about your language class, your teacher, your classmates, or whatever, is worth jotting down. Entries may be a sentence or two or several pages, depending on what's happening in your head at the time. As you make entries, date them. Then make a habit of looking back every few weeks at your entries.

It's a good idea to try to write something in your journal several times a week. Just take ten or fifteen minutes each time. At the very least, you should make an entry every week; any less frequently and you may lose trains of thought and find it hard to gain perspective on your progress.

The payoff for keeping a personal journal on your language learning journey will probably come sooner than you expect. The act of writing things down helps you to clarify your feelings, and if you're clear about your feelings you can deal with them better. Writing things down helps you to resolve certain issues and, if nothing else, to blow off steam. By reflecting on your language learning experience, you'll probably be able to sort out what's working for you and what isn't as you try different strategies. With a bit of luck, you'll really be able to see your progress in this journey!

For your first entry, try this: briefly describe your emotions as you start the semester. Here are some ideas.

Are you confident or unsure of yourself?
Are you excited or resigned?
Do you like your teacher?
Do you like the makeup of the class?
What do you think your feelings will be at the end of the semester?
    A feeling of accomplishment, or relief that it's over?

As you write, try to analyze why you feel the way you do and write those thoughts down.

CHAPTER TWO

Set Your Own Goals

One of the primary keys to success in any undertaking is to establish your own personal goals. The more those goals arise out of your convictions, beliefs, and general aspirations, the better are your chances of succeeding. If you're involved in something only because someone else has told you to be there, you're not as likely to come out a winner.

Why are you in this foreign language class? Maybe for years you've had a burning desire to master a certain language because you love the people, the country, or the heritage. Maybe your dream is to go and live where this language is spoken, and now is your chance to get a head start. Maybe you know that right here in this country there are good jobs in which your knowledge of a foreign language will be an asset. Or maybe you've fallen in love with that special someone whose language you now have exhilarating reasons to learn!

On the other hand, you may be here because a requirement says that's what you have to do to get a degree, and you're not too sure why "they" think it's so important to learn a foreign language. In that case, you may be secretly wishing you had some way to extricate yourself from this predicament. Right now, though, you'd settle for some good, positive, motivating goals to spur you on.

Wherever you stand right now in your perception of your personal goals for learning this language, your inner drive could be boosted a little, if not a lot, by looking carefully at just what this language can do for you. If you already have a strong drive to use this language for a particular purpose some day, then your job is relatively easy: you need to make sure your goals are clear in your mind and then pursue those goals vigorously!

If you find yourself in a grit-your-teeth and gut-your-way-through-it attitude, the best thing you can do for yourself right now is to discover the benefits you gain from plunging into this language with gusto.

It's true that just about everywhere you go in the world today you can find English Spoken Here signs. People in airports and taxis and hotels are able to meet your needs in the English language. But why should "we" rely on "them" to learn our language? The American tendency to be rather provincial in attitudes toward foreign languages has taken its toll in the world of trade and commerce. Partly because few Americans saw a purpose in learning "their" language, "they" came to us, learned our language, found out what we like and don't like, and sold us "their" products—in English.

Fortunately, there are some recent significant changes in our attitudes. Enrollments in foreign language classes have increased moderately in the last five years, dramatically so in Chinese, Japanese, and Russian. Some colleges and universities have reinstated their foreign language requirements. Lobby groups like the Joint National Committee for Languages are advocating legislation that favors funding of foreign language instruction. An Association to Cure Monolingualism has been founded to promote language teaching in the schools. And, most importantly, methods and materials for teaching foreign languages are improving.

Amidst these changes, there are some excellent practical reasons for you to learn a foreign language:[1]

- The U.S. government employs over 30,000 persons a year with a working knowledge of foreign languages.

- The State Department considers foreign language skills highly desirable for senior promotions.

- Many U.S. airlines favor those applicants who have foreign language skills.

- More than 850 radio stations in the U.S. broadcast in 58 foreign languages.

- About half of all U.S. multinational company executives know foreign languages.

- The Chase Manhattan Bank does more recruiting at the Georgetown Center for Strategic and International Studies than it does at Harvard Business School.

- A survey of 1,200 companies in the U.S. reported over 60,000 positions requiring employees with a knowledge of a foreign language.

- Major U.S. companies routinely employ 500 to 5,000 persons in other countries.

As you think about your personal goals for learning a foreign language, consider several deep-seated psychological and emotional needs that can be met:

1. Everyone has a need for *exploration* of the unknown, to see the "other side of the mountain." A language is both the unknown itself as well as an exciting means to reach unknown countries. Through a foreign language you can gain an awareness of other cultures and of other ways of thinking, feeling, and acting. Your whole perspective on life is significantly expanded through your foreign language.

2. We all need to have *stimulation* from other people, from our surroundings, or simply from new ideas. A foreign language is a powerful stimulus. As you figure out this brand new system of thinking, feeling, and acting, your mental powers are challenged. Your response (of wholeheartedly tackling this language) is rewarded through new contacts

---

[1]Data were provided by the Joint National Committee for Languages, Washington, D.C., March, 1986.

and new experiences. In addition, you'll probably end up learning more about how your own language works.

3. Everyone needs some form of *ego gratification*. That is, you need to feel accepted, appreciated, and valued by others. A foreign language adds one more important skill to your existing repertoire, one more reason to feel good about yourself. It allows you to operate in a bigger world than the one of your native language. Just wait until you find yourself in a foreign country where you can actually accomplish things in the foreign language! Believe me, as minor as it may seem to you now, that little thrill of victory is worth all the effort.

Do such factors help you to be more specific in perceiving your goals? If you had doubts before about what you can gain from learning a language, have some of those doubts now vanished?

As you go through the second week of your foreign language class, do the exercises below. If you'll do them faithfully (and they're not all that hard), you should begin to feel one of two things: (1) if you already have a good sense of why you want to learn a language, your goals will be refined so that you'll perceive them more clearly; (2) if you have some doubts about what your goals are or should be, you'll feel a sense of purpose motivating you to forge ahead. The clarity of your purpose will get you mentally and emotionally poised to take on the task that lies before you.

Exercises for Week Two

1. Try to visualize yourself out there somewhere actually using the language for communication (speaking, listening, reading, or writing it). Create as vivid a picture of yourself as you can. Describe it in your journal. Where are you? Who are you with? What context are you in? Now, hold on to that picture of yourself throughout this week. The picture may change scenes from time to time; that's okay. Just keep creatively visualizing yourself as an efficient, fluent language user, and make that your goal!

2. What are your personal goals in learning a foreign language? Write them down in your journal. If you have trouble thinking specifically here, review the list of contexts in which a foreign language is useful (page 6) and see if you're inspired by any of those.

You may want to review your goals in a few weeks to see if they still hold. It's quite normal to change your outlook as you progress, but it's important to focus on some goals right now.

3. Ask yourself how important it is for you to learn a foreign language. Be honest with yourself. If you lean toward feeling the process is not very important, try to figure out why you feel the way you do. See if you can increase the importance of language learning in your mind's eye by talking to your teacher and others about how you feel. Solicit their suggestions. If it's easy for you to grasp the importance of this language in your life, verbalize your goals anyway. That will help to keep your focus crystal clear.

4 . Think about the three categories that were mentioned in this chapter.

> the need for exploration
> the need for stimulation
> the need for ego gratification

See if you can find supportive reasons within each that might help you define goals. How will learning this language help you to explore? To be stimulated? To feel good about yourself? Record your thoughts in your journal.

CHAPTER THREE

Born to Win

> People who decide to become more of a winner than a loser . . . discover that they can rely, more and more, on their own capacities. . . . They continue to discover and renew themselves. For them, life consists not in getting more but in being more. Winners are glad to be alive!
>
> --Muriel James & Dorothy Jongeward, *Born to Win*[2]

You usually don't have to look very far to find someone who has the knack for languages, someone who picks up the flow of the language easily and seems to be able to converse in the language before anyone else. Some people seem to be born with a natural ability. They don't appear to have to work at the language very hard.

There may be one or two of these geniuses in your own foreign language class. They're always ready with the right answer to a question. They volunteer to speak often, and their hunches are almost always right. You sit across from them or behind them, admiring their apparent facility with the language, and you wonder why things don't come as easily for you.

By now you may be looking at the enormity of the task that's ahead of you. You've gotten through the first couple of weeks of your class and maybe things are going okay. But up ahead you see all kinds of rules and words and expressions that you've got to cram into your brain. Worse, you've got to *use* the stuff: the teacher will want you to speak, listen accurately, read, and maybe even write a little!

A foreign language is so complex a skill that self-confidence is one of the most important keystones for your success. Don't kid yourself. You're not going through this class just to add a few nonsense sounds and rules to your existing knowledge. This journey has ups and downs, rapids to run, rivers to ford, narrow trails to negotiate, and mountains to climb.

Learning a new language involves

- learning a whole new system of sounds that you have to make with the muscles of your tongue, mouth, and throat.
- internalizing thousands of new words that symbolize things, ideas, feelings, and actions.
- grasping countless rules and principles that govern how you can glue those words together to make sentences (we call this learning grammar).

---

[2]Muriel James and Dorothy Jongeward, *Born to Win* (Reading, MA: Addison-Wesley, 1976), p. 13.

- knowing even more rules on how those sentences are strung together into paragraphs, stories, information, conversations, and books.
- absorbing practical knowledge about what sorts of words and sentences are appropriate for one occasion and not appropriate for another—or, learning how to avoid sticking your foot in your mouth.
- understanding the culture of the people who speak the language and how their customs and habits differ from yours; without this understanding you may not be able to survive in their culture.

It's quite possible you feel that you're up to the task, that by slowly chipping away at this language, you'll grasp all these bits and pieces. If so, great! Just don't lose that self-confidence! On the other hand, you might be experiencing some self-doubt right about now, wondering if you can really do it. Will you be able to develop a knack of your own? Will you meet the challenge?

The answer to these questions is yes. Yes, you can learn a foreign language.

Think about these facts:

1. Little children almost universally pick up foreign languages without even realizing what they're doing.

2. Teenagers and adults who go to live in foreign countries are successful in learning the language as long as they really want to establish friendships with the people of the country.

3. Research has shown that it doesn't take an especially high IQ in order to learn a foreign language well. People of ordinary intelligence learn languages successfully.

4. In many parts of the world it's common for people to be bilingual. So there's nothing in learning a second language that's necessarily against basic nature.

What can you do to build your confidence? First of all, you should recognize that you have an overall sense of self-confidence; you feel good about yourself in general. You've made it this far in school. You've developed some special skills of your own—sports, playing an instrument, a hobby, or whatever. You've cultivated numerous friends over the years. You probably have some general career goals that you're pursuing now. In other words, you're a winner.

This general, overall good feeling about yourself is called *global self-confidence*. Don't lose sight of your global self-confidence. If at times you feel inadequate as you fumble through an attempt to say something, remember that this is a feeling you only get right here in your language class and not in general "out there."

You have to be prepared to feel a bit foolish as you try to say the right things; your classmates may even grow a little impatient. It's a humbling experience to go into a foreign language class after a dozen years of schooling and find that you know basically nothing! All the knowledge you gained in those years doesn't seem to help much. You have to start from square one.

Think about some of the foreign students who come to study in the U.S.A. They may be attending classes with you. Here they are, the cream of the crop back in Japan or Indonesia or Venezuela, the top five or ten percent of their graduating classes, competitively screened for study here and carefully selected by American colleges. These students often end up in an English as a Second Language (ESL) class designed to help them gain a level of English ability that will enable them to compete with their American classmates. Their global self-confidence miraculously remains intact, but their *specific self-confidence* (how they view themselves only in terms of their English proficiency) can be shattered. Their strong sense of global self-confidence, their belief that they can indeed do it, carries them along and reminds them that they have not lost their intelligence.

You too can preserve your sense of self-confidence in the face of the adversity of foreign language learning. Don't lose sight of yourself as an intelligent and capable person. So you're sometimes lost when too much of the foreign language is being used in the classroom. No problem! Just relax and remember you're in good company.

Another thing you can do to help build self-confidence is to set goals (as suggested in the last chapter) and reward yourself for achieving them. Keep reminding yourself of the little things you're accomplishing. Pat yourself on the back for the ground you gain. It doesn't hurt to look back behind you every now and then. At the beginning of the journey, the trip looks too long and too tiring; you can't look ahead to *everything* that's out in front of you. Look ahead a little, just enough to know where your next landmark is, and heap praises on yourself for having come this far.

Exercises for Week Three

1. Look at the ten items below and answer each of them with a *yes* or a *no*, depending on how you feel about yourself most of the time.

1. I understand myself.
2. I trust myself.
3. I make good use of my time.
4. I enjoy people.
5. People like to be around me.
6. I am rarely intimidated by other people.
7. I am optimistic about the future.
8. I think for myself.
9. I am a healthy person.
10. I like myself.

If you answered at least six of the ten items with a *yes*, that's a good indication that you have a good solid level of global self-confidence. You're basically a winner and you should take that winning attitude into your language class.

If you answered five or fewer with a *yes*, it might be an indication that your global self-confidence is lower than it should or could be. Tests like this are not foolproof, though, so before drawing any general conclusions, take a standard self-esteem test (most college counseling offices will have such tests), and have it interpreted. Chances are, you have a lot more going for you than you may think.

2. In your journal, describe any situations in your foreign language class in which you've found yourself feeling some self-doubt. Try to analyze your feelings and figure out where they stem from. Do they stem from previous foreign language classes? From your academic ability in general?
Some possible sources of self-doubt:

good list

The teacher has corrected you several times.
Classmates have shown some frustration with you.
Classmates seem to be a step ahead of you.
You've worked on some aspect of a lesson and just can't get it.
You can't seem to correctly pronounce some sound or set of sounds.
You feel lost while others seem to be doing okay.

Now, tell yourself you're not going to let these things get to you, that you're a winner, and that you're up to the challenge!

3. Talk with one or two classmates and share any feelings of self-doubt that you might have. You may be comforted to know that you're not alone in your apprehensions. Don't feel funny about sharing your feelings of confidence, too. You may thus be able to help boost someone else's self-confidence.

4. Set some specific goals for this week (beyond the assigned work for the course). Make sure they're realistic goals that are not way beyond your capacity. For example, you could do the following:

 a. Learn five useful phrases for conversation.
 b. Practice the phrases with a classmate until you both feel very comfortable with the routine.
 c. Memorize twenty vocabulary words, using flash cards or whatever technique you wish.
 d. Plan to go see one movie in the foreign language, preferably with subtitles, so you can understand what's going on but get accustomed to hearing the language.
 e. Spend a certain number of minutes daily—beyond what you usually spend with assigned homework—specifically working on the language.

5. Keep telling yourself: "I'm a winner. I can do it."

CHAPTER FOUR

Don't Worry!

The headline read, "Doing math is an emotional experience." The article was about a common ailment: math anxiety. One person was quoted as saying, "If you want to see me panic, all you have to say is, 'If two men dig a ditch in one hour . . .'" Another confessed, "When I see figures, I immediately feel I can't do it. . . . I just panic, block, freeze up."[3]

Math is in many ways like a foreign language. In both cases there are new systems, codes, rules, and ways of thinking that you have to get used to. So, foreign language anxiety and math anxiety share many of the same symptoms. It's easy to feel overwhelmed by all this new stuff that you have to learn. You've gotten so accustomed to thinking and expressing yourself in English that this new language just throws you. So you have a hard time relaxing in your foreign language class because there's very little there that you can depend on from your past experience. In other skills, from skiing to guitar playing, you have a lifetime of experiences to back you up. In a foreign language, you don't.

Sometimes anxiety comes from the classroom itself. You may be forced to focus on grammar rules, to memorize dialogues and vocabulary items, to translate from one language to the other, and to write grammar exercises. Throughout this maze of tasks, you feel defensive because you feel you must be ready to respond correctly when the teacher calls on you.

How can foreign language anxiety be avoided?

First, if you're motivated by your own goals (Chapter 2) and feel confident in your ability to meet the challenge (Chapter 3), you're halfway to eliminating anxiety. Anxiety is the fear—or, in a milder form, apprehension—that you will for one reason or another fail, make a fool of yourself, or do less than what you think is your best. You don't want to look bad with the rest of the class focusing on you. The key to allaying that fear is maintaining the self-confidence that you worked on last week. If you continue to feel you're a winner. then you'll be able to cope with, and lessen, anxiety.

Second, try not to engage in defensive learning. Too much of the time we get conditioned to compete against our classmates. We feel we have to fight off others to earn one of the few A grades that might be handed out. We learn to defend ourselves against the teacher and classmates. The language classroom is the worst possible place to do this defensive learning. Language should be used for communication, for cooperation, for negotiation, for harmony. Your classmates are your allies, your conversation partners, your tutors, your friends. Try to look at your classroom as a place where these friends can support one another.

---

[3]Barbara Utley, "Doing Math is an Emotional Experience," *Ann Arbor News*, 9 November 1978, p. B-1.

Third, don't get into negative thinking. Some people find foreign languages difficult because they're conditioned to believe that languages are difficult. People say:

"French was impossible!"
"I hated German, it was super hard."
"I was always lost in my Russian class."
"You'll never get it!"

But you don't have to let self-fulfilling prophecies take hold of you. Your best bet is to ignore any bad press. Don't let others' failures (for reasons that may not apply to you at all) convince you that you're not going to make it.

On the other hand, don't carry the illusion that your new language is going to be a piece of cake. A foreign language is a very difficult system to learn, and it's possible that a little bit of anxiety simply can't be avoided. But instead of letting those little bits of anxiety discourage you, just figure that a few little butterflies in the stomach from time to time are actually helpful. There is research that shows that "facilitative" anxiety is to be expected in many situations.

Think back to the last time you gave a little presentation in a class—any class. You may have felt a little nervous beforehand, but not so nervous that you fell apart. That little nervousness was facilitative anxiety. It was your body's way of telling you you were emotionally charged and ready to do your best. So the next time you feel a little fluttering in the midsection, tell yourself you're just about to do a great job.

Exercises for Week Four

1. Do you have any overall fears about learning a foreign language? If so, describe them in your journal. Just what is it, exactly, that you fear? What is the origin of this fear? (Some learners have noted that they can't stand the feeling of being lost, or of being laughed at, or of failing.) Try to resolve here and now that you simply won't allow yourself to be afraid of those things in this class.

2. Another journal assignment: describe the worst possible scenario you can imagine in the classroom. For example, you get humiliated by the teacher; the students all laugh at you; you get an F in your first quiz; every time you get called on, you give the wrong answer. Now share this scenario with a classmate or with several classmates, and get them to share their worst cases. You may find that you all laugh so hard *with* each other that your fears vanish. The real class sessions aren't half as bad as your worst-case scenarios.

3. Describe any specific instances in your class when you felt anxious or afraid. Did you choke up? Panic? Why did you feel that way? Is it possible that your anxiety could have become "facilitative"?

4. From your journal entry last week, review some of your discoveries about your global self-confidence. Can your global self-confidence spill over into lessening any anxieties that you may have?

5 . Do you engage in any defensive learning in your foreign language classroom? Why? Is there any alternative? Is the whole classroom atmosphere too defensive? If so, talk to your teacher about your feelings and ask him or her if there are any classroom activities that would help to get class members to pull together more.

6 . How do you feel now, compared to the first week of class, about your classroom environment? Is it supportive? threatening? How do you feel about your teacher? Can you share your thoughts with your teacher? If not, talk with some classmates and see if they feel the way you do.

7 . If you have any potential self-fulfilling prophecies within you that are giving you a bad attitude, describe them in your journal. Try to figure out what you can do to develop a winning attitude. Share your thoughts with your teacher and/or some classmates.

CHAPTER FIVE

Take the Plunge!

> One of the most wonderful feelings I have experienced in my study of a foreign language is being able to accept the fact that I'm always off balance. Somehow I have been able to suspend my usual demands on myself for immediate academic sureness. This has allowed me to enjoy myself, let go of some inhibitions about being wrong, and feel freer to experiment with the language.
>
> --from a foreign language learner's journal

You're now about five weeks into your foreign language course. If you've been following the exercises here with some success, you've thought quite a bit about why you want to succeed at learning this language, about how you can muster the self-confidence to do so, and about how to throw off some of that anxiety that only gets in the way.

Your five weeks of coursework have no doubt also gotten you into this language more deeply now. So, if you haven't already done so, now's the time to take the plunge! Dive into this language head first. How do you do that?

The first step in diving in is to make a concentrated effort to listen to the language. Listening gives you the opportunity to get used to the sounds, rhythm, and flow of the language without feeling you're on display. You've probably already been encouraged by your teacher to do a fair amount of speaking in class. That's okay, and it's good for you to get the muscles of your mouth to form the sounds of the language. But you shouldn't worry in these first few weeks about your speaking ability. Instead, concentrate on listening intently to the language. You might then find that you're less anxious about speaking the language because you've begun to get the sense of the language with your ears.

The first step, then, in taking the plunge, is to make a concentrated effort to listen to the language. This doesn't mean just listening in class. It means listening outside of class on your own, as your own self-assigned homework. (See Exercises 1 and 2 for this week.)

The second step in taking this plunge into the language is to start talking. Language learning requires risk taking. It is necessary for you to be as bold and uninhibited as possible. You simply have to risk saying things that aren't quite right, and be thick-skinned enough not to let it bother you.

In order to take the plunge, you have to fight your normal inclination, which is to protect yourself. You'll do anything not to appear foolish and stupid. Even if you know words or phrases that are correct, you may feel that trying to pronounce this foreign language accurately will make your classmates laugh at you. You want to avoid exposing your weaknesses.

So what happens? You clam up. When you do get brave, you risk very little by sticking with language forms that you're already sure of. You play it safe. You want to just fall in with the crowd and not be noticed too much. Obviously, these tactics aren't going to help you to dive into the language. You simply must convince yourself that mistakes aren't signs of weakness or failure. They're natural patterns of learning.

One learner who became very proficient in English, largely through a technique that required an extremely uninhibited attitude, was Hans Durbeek. Durbeek, from Holland, reported that as a young boy of 14 he made a regular practice of rehearsing make-believe conversations in English as he walked to and from school. He said the other kids thought he was a little strange, constantly talking to himself. But he persisted in his practice, and became the most proficient English speaker in his school. Twenty years later, he was almost indistinguishable from a native speaker of English. Granted, his self-rehearsed role plays were not the only contributing factor, but his technique is an excellent illustration of taking the plunge.

In the 1970s, a study done at the University of Michigan concluded that small amounts of alcohol induce a lowering of inhibitions which, in turn, may help learners to do a better job of pronouncing a foreign language. Those of us who worked at Michigan at the time had some fun facetiously recommending that Michigan's foreign language departments include champagne in what was definitely a beer budget!

Of course, you don't need alcohol to lower your inhibitions and defenses. What you need is a good dose of self-confidence and fellow learners who respect each other and recognize how vulnerable each person is. When you all understand that you're in this together, you can start accepting one another's little weaknesses, and try saying things even though they may be wrong.

One time some kids from the local high school French club happened to knock on my door, hoping for a little donation for their activities. As soon as I learned they were from the French club I broke into my own less than perfect French: "Ah, c'est très bien, alors. Vous parlez français! S'il vous plaît, entrez. Nous pouvons parler français un petit peu?" Upon hearing a barrage of what they faintly recognized as French, they looked at each other, embarrassed, then looked back at me, and quickly—in English—thanked me for my interest and left! They weren't about to reveal that French 1A in the local high school had hardly prepared them to enter into even the most elementary conversation with a real person. The risk in such an attempt would have been too devastating.

But your risks can be calculated. Studies have shown that people can be categorized as high, moderate, and low risk takers. Guess which ones have the best success index? The moderate risk-takers. In other words, you can be wild and frivolous in your attempts at guessing, or, on the other hand, you can be too protective of your ego. A low risk-taker's percentage of guesses may be better, but the rate of progress is much, much slower. Nothing ventured, nothing gained.

Your goal, then, should be to develop a pattern of moderate risk taking so that you can play the odds. You can afford to be a little audacious, but by the same token don't always be the one to blurt out an answer or to engage in incessant fractured blather in the second language. Hold back enough to do some figuring about appropriate moments to speak. Try to become a calculated risk-taker. Good language learners are willing but accurate guessers.

Exercises for Week Five

1. Make specific efforts to find audiotapes, videotapes, and movies in the language. Many video rental stores now feature a section on foreign films. Look for films in your foreign language and check them out. Make sure they're subtitled, not dubbed; subtitled films provide auditory input in the foreign language. As you watch movies or tapes, or as you play audiotapes, listen carefully for meaning. Play the tapes over and over as many times as you wish, and keep listening for meaning, for words you recognize, for phrases you've already learned. At the same time, try to relax as bit and let the overall sound patterns and expressions in this language soak in.

2. If possible, team up with one or more of your classmates to watch foreign films. As you're watching, you can help each other to recognize elements of the language. Use your rewind and playback button liberally!

3. Are you a high, moderate, or low risk-taker, in general? Comment in your journal on how you see yourself on such a scale. If you think you're too low a risk-taker, try to take a few more risks in class.

   If you find yourself getting too bold in this risk taking business (which for many isn't likely!), try to figure out how you might resist blurting things out in the language. In other words, see if you can make your risks as calculated as possible.

4. Have there been times where you've held back from saying something in class because you weren't sure exactly what to say? What would have happened if you had taken the plunge then? If you can think of a specific instance, describe it in your journal and speculate on what the repercussions, if any, would have been.

5. In a bookstore, find a tourist phrase book in your foreign language. Look at some of the common phrases used for greetings and introductions, for ordering a meal at a restaurant, or for finding your way through a city. Practice some of the phrases with a partner from your class. You could even attempt some role playing. Try to sound as much like a native speaker of the foreign language as you can. Don't give up on this technique after a few attempts. It may take a while for the phrases to roll off your tongue.

6. Find a proficient speaker of the language you're learning. It could be a friend, a relative, or a person in an advanced course. Set aside some time to carry on conversations with this person. How do you feel?

CHAPTER SIX

Wide-Angle Lenses, Please

Take a little journey back in time. Pretend that you're about five years old. Notice that you're quite fluent in your own language. You're able to ask for things you want, to respond to other kids and adults when they want things from you, to express frustration, anger, happiness. In short, with your native language you can do just about anything your five-year-old mind wants to.

But how much do you know *about* this language? How aware are you of the fact that you're actually using something called "language"?

Kids are unaware of the language they are using. Up to the age of five or so, children don't think at all about the rules that govern language. They will, of course, ask questions about what a word means ("Dad, what does 'respect' mean?"), or they will ask for clarification ("Huh?"). But they're not interested in—or capable of grasping the significance of— language as a system governed by rules. They don't have the least bit of interest in grammar or correctness. They simply want to get at meaning.

A researcher once asked three-year-old Adam, "Now, Adam, listen to what I say. Which is better to say . . . *some* water, or . . . *a* water?" Adam nonchalantly replied, "Pop go weasel!" Adam wanted no part of this senseless inquisition!

In learning foreign languages, kids have this same innocent, "pop go weasel" unawareness of the bit and pieces of the language they're learning. They learn it naturally, without thinking about it. Intellectually, kids are somewhat relaxed. They make a game of language learning. They don't think about the rules that they're subconsciously using and modifying daily. Instead, they focus on the goals of language use: communication with others for specific purposes. Kids "pick up" language. They don't watch themselves the way adults in a classroom often do.

Should you, like a kid, try to pick up language subconsciously? The answer is a qualified yes. As an adult now, you most likely analyze yourself too much. Your tendency is to memorize, focus on grammar rules, translate from one language to the other, and do just about everything *except* subconsciously acquire it. You're probably learning facts about the language at the expense of learning to use it. And one sure way to fail at learning a foreign language is not to use it for genuine communication.

Learning a foreign language is like learning to play tennis (or any other sport). If you think about it too much, it won't work. Like other tennis players, I often used to overanalyze some aspect of my tennis game. I'd tell myself to watch the ball, or follow through on my stroke, or shift my grip for the backhand. Before I knew it, I was analyzing myself so much everything would fall apart. What I was doing was monitoring myself to the extent that I was too acutely aware of myself. At times like these, I finally found that I was better off just relaxing and not thinking about my tennis game. Instead, I was better served by simply focusing on my opponent, or on winning the game—anything but focusing on myself.

Or think of another analogy: would you try to learn how to swim without a swimming pool to swim in? Well, learning things about your foreign language in the classroom is a bit like trying to learn how to swim out of water. You can go through the motions, learn some of the theory, but sooner or later you have to jump in the water. And when that happens, you'd better just focus on staying afloat and crossing the pool, not on the rules of flotation.

So we adults should focus less on things *about* the language and more on purposes that our second language can accomplish. But should we shy away entirely from focusing here and there on small pronunciation problems, or on grammar, or on vocabulary or expressions? Certainly not. Here's one more analogy for those of you who aren't sports fans.

Language learning is like a camera with a variable lens on it. Most of the time when we're using language for communication, we ought to be using wide-angle lenses. We should be looking for the whole picture of what someone is trying to say or write. The problem is that our classroom environment tends to coax us into using a zoom lens almost all the time. We want to scrutinize language. We want to look at all the details. We want to know what every word means, how every rule is applied and what all their exceptions are. Our linguistic zoom lenses are turned to focus in on all the details, just when we should be using a wide-angle shot to take in as much meaning as possible.

Before you trade in your zoom lens entirely, however, remember that it's an important tool in helping you to see what you can't see with the wide-angle lens. As you're trying to take in this language, it's very useful to be able to quickly zoom in on a rule or an explanation that clarifies some problem area, then zoom back out to the wider angle.

We adults really have an advantage over kids here. We can use optimal focusing for our own good, and we're not limited to the time-consuming process of learning something subconsciously by discovery. Kids only have the wide-angle lens. We have both.

It's not too ridiculous to conclude, is it, that adults are potentially *superior* to children in foreign language learning? If we could only harness that ability! Research on successful language learners shows that a significant portion of adult success is attributable to optimal conscious learning. You need to be just childlike enough to relax with the language and not be overly worried about all of its details. But at the right moment, you need to be able to monitor yourself or your language with your zoom lens, then take corrective action.

In short, try not to think too much about your language learning process, but allow yourself optimal occasions to zoom in and figure out what's going on. If you can balance the two principles of focusing closely and of getting the larger picture, you will be well on your way to success.

Exercises for Week Six

1. Look at the following message. What does it say? Don't give up after just a minute or two. Play with it for awhile, even if you set it aside and come back to it later. Eventually you'll see it. (The answer is in the Appendix at the end of the book.)

This little puzzle is an example of how sometimes you focus on the wrong thing in a language, or how you don't back off enough to get a wide-angle view of language. If you look too closely at the message above, you overanalyze. If you back off, you'll get it. Language works the same way.

2. If you're anywhere near a young child who is learning a second language (the child could be an immigrant learning English), try to observe how the child goes about using the foreign language. What kind of shortcuts does the child use to get meanings across? How concerned is the child about correctness? Is the child able to compensate in some way for language that is lacking? In your journal, draw some analogies between what the child does and what you could be doing to make your language learning more efficient.

3. Another journal topic: assess the extent to which you think you may be *overmonitoring* yourself as you deal with the foreign language. Do you find yourself thinking about rules as you speak? Do you find that you have to hesitate a lot because you are trying to get it by the book?

4. One way to try to use a wide-angle lens in learning a language is to continue listening to your foreign language as often as possible, using some of the suggestions made in the exercises for Chapter 5. As you keep on listening to tapes, watching videos, or whatever, see if you can just catch overall meanings without getting hung up on specific words you don't know.

Now, do the same thing as you read something in the foreign language. Try to maintain an even pace as you read. Don't look up words you don't know; save that for later if a word or two seem crucial to your understanding. Try to grasp the overall meaning of the passage you read.

5 . Try this technique that some learners have used successfully at the beginning stages of language: as you're trying to say things in the foreign language, and you can't find the right word for something, just go ahead and substitute English words. Don't worry about the fact that it's not the correct foreign language word. (Note: Check this out with the teacher first to make sure you won't get chastised for this technique. Explain that you're using it as a strategy that you'll eventually discard.) Example:

> Je veux aller à la *shopping center* pour acheter quelques plumes et quelques *erasers*.

This technique is a bit unorthodox, but it could help you in the early stages to maintain the flow of language without overmonitoring your speech.

CHAPTER SEVEN

Cooperative Learning

Think about all the classes you've sat through since kindergarten. How much of your learning was a process of competing against others sitting in the same room with you, trying to outdo them in the grade-getting game? How much of your learning was taken up with pleasing your teachers, doing what they told you to do? And how much of your learning was a product of figuring out the school rules, the state requirements, and the standardized tests that attempted to assess your intelligence?

Too much of our learning in school tends to be defensive, a point that was brought out in Chapter 4. We learn to defend ourselves and our minds against the competition of other learners, the teacher, and the institution. This sets up motives for learning that are upside-down. Instead of learning for its benefits we keep up the pace just to avoid certain punishments.

The learning of a foreign language simply cannot be successful if you come to your classroom with a defensive approach. Language is a tool for communication, social bonding, cooperation, and understanding. It's unlikely that anyone ever learned a foreign language with highly defensive motivations. One of the reasons that college students often fail to become fluent in foreign language classes is that they're motivated for the wrong reasons. Their interest is in passing a requirement rather than in learning to use the language for practical reasons.

One way to ward off this defensive learning syndrome is to work cooperatively with your classmates and your teacher. Decide right now that the last thing you're going to do is worry about whether someone sitting next to you is going to do better than you. In fact, you might actively encourage your classmates and your teacher to pull together and do some group work. Help each other. One person's weakness may be another's strength. Don't concentrate on winning out against someone else in the class. In valuing your fellow learners, you will gain in the long run.

Treating your classmates and teacher as partners in this process of learning requires a little bit of extroversion on your part. If you enjoy working in a team with other people, if you like to have other people around you, if you prefer interacting with others to thinking things through privately, then you're probably naturally extroverted, and the job of working with others won't be a tough one at all.

Actually, extroversion is a widely misunderstood term. Many of us have been led to think that an extrovert is always the life of the party, the first to raise a hand in the classroom, the loud one who is armed with witty remarks for every occasion. But those behaviors could come from an introvert whose defenses are high. Extroversion, technically defined, is the need (and ability) to receive ego gratification and a sense of wholeness from other people. Introversion is the need and ability to derive this sense of self-esteem from within oneself.

Because American society tends to value gregariousness, those who raise their hands often and who participate willingly and frequently are generally highly valued and rewarded by teachers. Quiet, reserved behavior is sometimes viewed as passive behavior. Interestingly enough, other cultures often value just the opposite. The quiet, reserved student is thought of as being well-behaved and smart.

Extroversion is not always expressed by loud or assertive behavior. Extroverts simply need others as a mirror to see themselves. They derive their sense of happiness and fulfillment from being with other people and from receiving affirmation from other people. To receive that affirmation, extroverts don't always need to be in the limelight. They can just "be there."

On the other side of the coin, introversion is much too maligned in our culture. Introverts are simply able to find affirmation (which we all need) within themselves. They don't need as much contact with others. Yet the inner strength of an introvert is not often recognized. So if someone ever says, "You're a real introvert, aren't you?" you should take it as a compliment!

Do these ideas offer any insight into finding your pathway to foreign language success? If you're on the extroverted side, capitalize on your ability to derive fulfillment from being with others. Use the foreign language as much as possible as a vehicle for achieving that fulfillment. In a classroom, go ahead and ham it up a bit—but not to the point of being obnoxious, of course.

If, on the other hand, you prefer solitude and you're pretty comfortable working out solutions to problems on your own, then you'll have to stretch yourself a little to get out there and work in a partnership with some other members of the class. The stretch probably won't be traumatic. It's a matter of recognizing that the purpose of language is communication, so you might as well start now to communicate with others. The sooner you stick your neck out and get into the fray, the better.

Exercises for Week Seven

1. Take the following self-test and score yourself according to the directions at the end. You must circle either *a* or *b*, even if you have a hard time placing yourself into one or the other.

1. I usually like

    a. mixing with people
    b. working alone

2. I'm more inclined to be

    a. fairly reserved
    b. pretty easy to approach

3. I'm happiest when I'm

    a. alone
    b. with other people

4. At a party, I

     a. interact with many, including strangers
     b. interact with a few people I know

5. In my social contacts and groups, I usually

     a. get behind on the news
     b. keep abreast of what's happening with others

6. I can usually do something better by

     a. figuring it out on my own
     b. talking with others about it

7. My usual pattern when I'm with other people is

     a. to be open and frank, and to take risks
     b. to keep to myself and not be very open

8. When I make friends, usually

     a. someone else makes the first move
     b. I make the first move

9. I would rather

     a. be at home on my own
     b. go to a boring party

10. Interaction with people I don't know

     a. stimulates and energizes me
     b. taxes my reserves

11. In a group of people I usually

     a. wait to be approached
     b. initiate conversation

12. When I'm by myself I usually feel a sense of

     a. loneliness and uneasiness
     b. solitude and peacefulness

13. In a classroom situation I prefer

     a. group work, interacting with others
     b. individual work

14. When I get into a quarrel or argument, I prefer to

     a. be silent, hoping the issue will resolve itself or blow over
     b. "have it out" and settle the issue right then and there

15. When I try to put deep or complex thoughts into words, I usually

    a. have quite a hard time
    b. do so fairly easily

Scoring procedure:

Mark an X corresponding to your choices in the grid below:

	ⓐ	b		a	ⓑ		a	ⓑ
1			2			3		
4			5			6		
7			8			9		
10			11			12		
13			14			15		

TOTALS [ ] + [ ] + [ ] = [ ]

Add up the number of X's in ONLY three of the columns, as indicated. (Ignore all other X's.) Total those three numbers to get a grand total, and write it in the box at the right. This is your score for the test.
    Here's how to interpret your score:

13 and above: quite extroverted
9 to 12:   moderately extroverted
7 or 8:   moderately introverted
6 and below: quite introverted

What are the implications of this self-test for your language learning process?
    If you scored a nine or above, indicating that you're extroverted, try to capitalize on your need to be with others. Use that tendency to interact with people in the foreign language. Even if you aren't strong linguistically, you'll probably derive enough emotional strength from others that you'll keep trying. Group work in class should be your strength. However, being highly extroverted may mean that you don't do enough work on your own,

such as studying aspects of the language that give you difficulty, working on vocabulary items, and so forth. You may be almost too willing to plunge into the language without enough contemplation on how the system works.

If you're on the introverted side of the scoring range, your strength is probably in thinking through aspects of the language and working on grammar and vocabulary on your own. Use your enjoyment of solitude to sort out the mysteries of the language. At the same time, though, don't shy away from face-to-face communication, which you may be likely to do. Group work and free conversation in the language may scare you a bit, but if you can work in very small groups of two or three, your inhibitions will be less likely to hamper your efforts. The systematic thinking that you've done on your own will very likely pay off as you open up.

2 . In your journal, comment on the extent to which you feel that you're generally extroverted or introverted. Did this test bear out your gut feeling? See if you can write down some specific things you can do, in light of your extroversion level, to take advantage of your talents. Work on those things this week and in the following weeks.

3 . If you haven't yet done so, do this without any further delay: Among the friends and acquaintances in your foreign language class, try to find a small group of people—a conversation group—to practice your language with. If you can coax or hire someone proficient in the language to be your group's tutor, so much the better. But at least work on the principle that a small group can provide an ideal context for cooperative learning.

4 . Check your journal entry in Week 4 on defensive learning (Exercise 5). Do your feelings still hold true? Do you find that you've loosened up a bit and are now more wiling to cooperate with classmates? Keep trying to view your classmates as your allies, and not as competitors in a contest for grades.

5 . You're about halfway through the semester. Now might be a good time to look back through your journal and see if you:

- are more motivated than you were at the outset
- have developed more self-confidence in your language
- are less anxious than you were
- are more willing to take calculated risks
- can use a wide-angle linguistic lens most of the time but use a zoom lens to your advantage every now and then.

CHAPTER EIGHT

Discover Your Own Learning Styles

Suppose you're visiting a foreign country where you don't speak or read the language. You've landed in the airport, and your contact person, whose name you don't know, isn't there to meet you. To top it off, your luggage is missing. It's 3:00 A.M. and no one in the sparsely staffed airport speaks English. What would you do?

There's obviously no single solution to this irritating problem. Your solution will be based to a great extent on the problem-solving styles you happen to bring to bear. For example, if you're somewhat *tolerant of ambiguity*, you won't get easily flustered by your unfortunate circumstances. If you're *reflective*, you'll exercise patience and not jump quickly to a conclusion about how to approach the situation. If you're basically *right-brained*, you'll focus on the whole picture without being distracted by irrelevant details.

Learning styles are personal characteristics of thinking, analyzing, or problem solving that distinguish you from other people. We each have unique ways of taking in information, digesting it, and recalling it for later use. Differing learning styles are the primary reason that educational institutions have to pay attention to the individualization of instruction. We don't all learn things in the same way.

Learning styles and personality styles are related. Someone who is intellectually tolerant of ambiguity, for example, will often be personally open-minded and tolerant of differences among people. Learning styles act as a bridge between mind and emotion. The threads of intellect are closely woven into the fabric of personality. Nevertheless, learning styles shouldn't be thought of as being permanent and unchangeable. We can shape them, direct them, and control them just as we can mold personality characteristics. So a general tendency in style can be recognized as just that. If you find that your style might work against you in some way, you can, with some concentrated effort, change it for the particular task at hand.

In foreign language learning, there's no one set of styles that's necessarily right for everyone. Not everyone succeeds in the same way. Three decades of research on individual variation in language learning have proved that point.

As you discover how certain learning styles provide important keys to foreign language success, try to figure out what your own particular styles are. You'll then get a sense of how you can capitalize on your uniqueness and develop your own personal pathway to success.

Now, before you read on, stop here and take the test in Exercise 1 at the end of this chapter (page 34).

Coping with chaos How do you cope when things get confusing and chaotic? Do you usually panic and search for an immediate way to extricate yourself from the situation? Or do you more calmly accept confusion, figuring that eventually there will be a way to account for it all? The answers to these questions may tell you how you should go about tackling a foreign language. Research has shown that people who are generally *tolerant of ambiguity* are usually better language learners than those who tend to be more *intolerant of ambiguity*.

Ambiguity simply refers to all those ideas, thoughts, feelings, problems, rules, and theories that you don't fully understand. You're surrounded by ambiguity all the time. Information and feelings may be unclear or vague. Concepts don't always fall into place in your meaningful mental structures; for example, you may not fully grasp a political issue, a scientific law, a chemical formula, a social philosophy, or how a microwave oven works. Communication events are also part of the sea of ambiguity that you have to navigate daily. You have to make sense out of what you read in the newspaper, what a salesperson tries to push on you, or what sort of a career to pursue. Often these aren't simple little problems.

Most of the time, you want everything to fit into a neatly ordered framework. Your general learning style—your intellectual or emotional tolerance level—will determine how you handle ambiguity. Some people need to have clear answers for all issues, however muddy those issues may be. Such people tend to be categorical; they want to see the universe in black and white with no shades of gray. At the other extreme are people who are more flexible and tend to allow for many models of truth.

Ambiguity tolerance is much like the old holding patterns around busy airports. A plane may not be able to land right at the moment, but it isn't sent away or rejected just because it doesn't fit in right now. It's allowed to circle, and in due time, the control tower will let it land.

How do you handle the ambiguity of learning a second language? What about all those words you don't know? Rules you haven't grasped? Social niceties that escape you? Most of us tend to be too intolerant when we learn a second language. We want everything to fit into familiar patterns, usually those of our native language. You need to get beyond that resistance in second language learning. Don't let everything that you don't know or don't understand get you down. Don't yield to the temptation to throw it all out just because it doesn't fit. After all, your mind is like a parachute; it only works when it's open.

You may be asking, just how do you put the ambiguous stuff into some sort of mental holding pattern? The answer is, by understanding your own limits and not trying to get everything crammed into your head all at once. Take it a step at a time. Find your own pace. If you've tried to understand some grammatical point but it doesn't sink in, let it go for a few days and come back to it. If those fifty words you're supposed to learn this week are too much, cut the list down into small chunks and learn them gradually. But above all, don't let all this confusion throw you for a loop. If you are patient and diligent, things will eventually sink in.

Gambling for language Are you a slow or a fast reader? Are you usually the first one to put your hand up and speak out in a classroom? or the last? Do you like to make sure you're right before venturing a thought, or would you just as soon make a lot of little guesses, some of which might be wrong? Another learning style in which people tend to lean toward one side or the other is *impulsivity* and *reflectivity*, sometimes referred to as *gambling* versus *non-gambling* styles.

A reflective style favors a slower, more methodical approach to problems. Reflective people tend to have a need to be certain of solutions before venturing possibilities. They're the tortoises of the world, who slowly but steadily move ahead in sure, logical steps. They're usually slower readers, who want to make sure that they grasp what they're reading before moving on. Consequently, they'll make fewer errors in reading.

Impulsive learners, on the other hand, are faster thinkers. They make good mental gamblers because gambling often requires quick thinking and reliance on following one's hunches. Gamblers have to be willing to be wrong sometimes. They tend to be fast readers since they're usually willing to overlook words, phrases, and thoughts that they don't immediately grasp, in favor of moving on. While they'll make more errors in reading, they have usually mastered the "guessing game" of reading well enough that overall comprehension isn't impaired.

How you handle the pitfalls and benefits on both sides of the continuum will make a difference in the success you'll have in learning a second language. It's easy to see how too much reflectivity would work against you. Many second language learners are too reflective when they speak a second language. They struggle laboriously through long pauses of searching for the right word or inflection before moving on through a sentence. A bit of impulsivity would help such learners. Be careful, though, because too much impulsivity can work against you. As you blurt out one language "hypothesis" after another, fracturing your language beyond recognition, you may not properly develop a system within your brain.

So, you need to be balanced in your approach. Somewhere between too much reflectivity and too much impulsivity lies a happy medium where you can be successful in your learning. In this optimal zone, you have the guts to try out your hunches, but you temper your attempts with some reflection.

Now, do Exercises 2 and 3 at the end of this chapter (page 35) before continuing with the next section here.

Eyes or ears? A third learning style preference is one that you're no doubt already quite aware of: *visual* (a preference for *seeing* information) versus *auditory* (a preference for *hearing* information). Your score on the self-test in Exercise 3 may indicate your general preference toward visual or auditory input. It also may be off-base; brief tests like this are not always completely on target. In that case, use your intuition to determine whether you're more visual, more auditory, or equally divided in your learning preferences.

As a foreign language learner, you can help find your pathway to success by recognizing your generally preferred way of learning and then by treating yourself to as much input as possible in your preferred style. If you like seeing words written down, pictures, and charts, and you're not getting enough of that, seek out such input. If you're not getting enough auditory input—hearing the sounds of the language, hearing directions, listening to other speakers—do something to load up on that side.

Sometimes teachers conduct their classes in styles that run counter to your basic preferences. Is there anything you can do about that? A good start would be to ask your teacher's opinion on what may be good or bad for your ultimate learning success. You have to remember, of course, that everyone in your class has a different style of learning and not everyone can be equally pleased. So you may need to take your learning goals firmly into your own hands by understanding your learning style preferences and doing something about it. The remaining exercises (4 and 5) in this chapter, along with those in the next chapter, should give you a boost in taking learning into your own hands.

Exercises for Week Eight

1. In each item of the test below, circle the response that best describes you. If you strongly agree that a statement describes you, circle *YES!*. If you strongly disagree, circle *NO!*. If you basically or mildly agree or disagree, then circle *yes* or *no,* respectively. If you're neutral, circle *?*. In each item, refer to the foreign language that you're now learning.

a. I am bothered when I don't understand everything in the foreign language.   YES!   yes   ?   no   NO!

b. I like to know specific rules for all aspects of grammar.   YES!   yes   ?   no   NO!

c. I am uncomfortable with just a vague understanding of conversations in which I am a participant.   YES!   yes   ?   no   NO!

d. Multiple or hidden meanings in the foreign language confuse me.   YES!   yes   ?   no   NO!

e. I avoid reading material in the foreign language that I don't understand.   YES!   yes   ?   no   NO!

f. I like my foreign language class to be structured so that I know just what is going to happen next.   YES!   yes   ?   no   NO!

g. Starting to learn a new foreign language is scary.   YES!   yes   ?   no   NO!

To score the test, assign numbers to each circled answer as follows:

YES!	yes	?	no	NO!
1	2	3	4	5

Write your score for each item in the margin to the right of the text. Then, total all seven numbers. Interpretation:

Suzanne Scott

25 and above:	quite tolerant of ambiguity in the foreign language
21 to 24:	mildly tolerant
17 to 20:	mildly intolerant
16 and below:	quite intolerant

If you're on the tolerant side of the continuum of possibilities (21 and above), you should find that you remain reasonably level-headed in the face of the chaos of your foreign language. Keep that tolerance level high, and it will save you from getting overwhelmed. Just make sure you don't get so laid back that nothing ever "comes in for a landing."

If your score is on the intolerant side (17 or below), you should consider making it a personal goal to learn to put certain unknowns on hold while you just keep moving on. Take things a step at a time. If a few things slip by you, try not to worry about it. The advantage you hold, of course, is that you tend to keep the pressure on to make everything fit together. Don't lose that motivation; just tone it down a bit.

Now, go back to the section "Coping with chaos" (page 32).

2 . There are no succinct tests of reflectivity/impulsivity that can be used in a valid way here. Instead, assess yourself in this learning style. Look at yourself as you interact in the foreign language classroom. Do you volunteer to speak more than the average student? Less? Or are you right in there with the average student? When you speak do you hesitate a lot? Are there long pauses while you try to think of what you should say? Or do you more or less blurt it out?

If you're a more reflective learner, and you think it's holding you back from participating in class or from speaking the language in general, start now to participate more even if you aren't always sure you're right. If you're more impulsive in your style, ask yourself whether you think you're at an appropriate level of impulsivity, which you may well be. In that case, continue to participate freely. But if you think you're too impulsive and could benefit by "looking before you leap," then try some of that in the classroom.

3 . In the test[4] below, circle *a*, *b*, or *c*.

    a. I understand directions better when
        a. the teacher tells them to me
        b. I read them
        c. no preference either way

    b. I learn better when I
        a. hear material from the teacher
        b. read what the teacher writes on the chalkboard
        c. no preference

---

[4]Adapted from Joy M. Reid, "The Learning Style Preferences of ESL Students," *TESOL Quarterly* 21 (March 1987): pp. 87-111.

c. I understand explanations of concepts better when I
    a. hear them
    b. read them
    c. no preference

d. I remember words better when I
    a. hear them spoken out loud
    b. see them in writing
    c. no preference

e. I prefer
    a. listening to lectures
    b. reading a textbook
    c. no preference

f. I prefer
    a. to hear a story
    b. to read a story
    c. no preference

g. I remember
    a. sounds better
    b. pictures better
    c. no preference

Scoring: number of *a* answers: _____ (*auditory*)

                number of *b* answers: _____ (*visual*)
                (*Don't count (c) answers.*)
                If *a* is larger, you prefer *auditory* learning
                If *b* is larger, you prefer *visual* learning

If you're an auditory learner, there may be some things you could do to give yourself an edge. Use more tapes. Pay maximum attention to the input of the teacher and the other students in class. Use sound-alike words or rhyming words to remember vocabulary. If you like visual learning, try to maximize your visual input. Write words and sentences down. Draw charts. Remember words by associating them with pictures.

Now, go back to the section "Eyes or ears?"

4. Many of the emotional factors that you looked at in previous chapters contribute to your overall learning style preferences. Now is a good time to look back over those chapters and, in your journal, assess yourself in terms of some of the topics covered. Here are some questions to ask yourself:

a. Do I create motivation to learn the language?
b. Do I believe strongly in myself?
c. Do I try to reduce anxiety and fear?
d. Am I a willing risk-taker?
e. Do I try to get the "big picture"?

f. Do I cooperate with (and not compete against) my classmates?
g. Do I engage in self-evaluation of my progress?
h. Do I set up opportunities to practice the language?
i. Do I set long-term and short-term goals?

If your answer is yes to all of the above, you're well on your way to developing successful channels for language learning.

5. With a partner or small group from your class, compare notes on the three learning styles covered in this chapter (ambiguity tolerance, reflectivity/impulsivity, and auditory/visual preference). You may discover that you differ from others, but that you all can be equally successful with your differing approaches. Record, in your journal, your reactions to this comparing session.

CHAPTER NINE

Balance Your Brain

Sixteen-year-old Alex had lived in Yugoslavia all his life when he, with his family, decided to emigrate to the United States. However, the family had to remain one year in France before moving to New York. During that year Alex systematically focused on the English language, rather than French, and in an untiring effort, studied the sound system of English. He read books on phonetics and English linguistics and listened to records and tapes designed to teach English pronunciation. Usually outgoing and friendly, Alex didn't socialize with French people to any appreciable extent during that year.

At last the day came when Alex arrived in New York. He made Brooklyn his home. Elated with the new surroundings, he immediately put his studies and his gregarious nature to work. He talked with Americans at every opportunity and worked in restaurants where he also practiced speaking, and during this time never touched his phonetics books or records. Three years later, at the age of twenty, he became a student at the University of Illinois and was the subject of a case study on foreign language learning.

As the researcher played tapes of Alex's speech in a graduate seminar, those of us in the class were fooled: we swore we were listening to a guy who was born and bred in Brooklyn! Alex had so authentically picked up the dialect of his three-year environment that we could scarcely discern a foreign accent!

Your journey to fluency may not be as dramatic. But it could easily incorporate elements of Alex's secret of success. He was able to incorporate the functions of both "left brain" and "right brain" into his successful learning of English.

At this point, before reading on, do Exercise 1 for this chapter (page 41). Don't read on until you have done that exercise!

There is evidence available now that the two sides, or *hemispheres*, of the human brain each have special functions to perform. The left hemisphere is associated with logical, analytical thought, and with mathematical and linear processing of information. The right hemisphere perceives and remembers visual, tactile, and auditory images, and is more efficient in processing holistic, integrative, and emotional information. The differences between left- and right-brain functioning comprise a whole set of style differences.

The chart below[5] lists characteristics of left- and right-brain functioning. Many of these characteristics were included in the test in Exercise 1.

Left-Brain Dominance	Right-Brain Dominance
Intellectual	Intuitive
Remembers names	Remembers faces
Responds to verbal instructions and explanations	Responds to demonstrated, illustrated or symbolic instructions
Experiments systematically and with control	Experiments randomly and with less restraint
Makes objective judgements	Makes subjective judgments
Planned and structured	Fluid and spontaneous
Prefers established, certain information	Prefers elusive, uncertain information
Analytical reader	Synthesizing reader
Reliance on language in thinking and remembering	Reliance on images in thinking and remembering
Prefers talking and writing	Prefers drawing and manipulating objects
Prefers multiple choice tests	Prefers open-ended questions
Controls feelings	More free with feelings
Not good at interpreting body language	Good at interpreting body language
Rarely uses metaphors	Frequently uses metaphors
Favors logical problem solving	Favors intuitive problem solving

In recent years there's been a flurry of interest in left- and right-brain functioning. Books like Betty Edwards' *Drawing on the Right Side of the Brain*,[6] for example, got some attention from would-be artists who didn't fare well with left-brained methods of imaging and visualizing their subject matter. In Japan, Tsunoda's *The Japanese Brain*[7] asserted the uniqueness of hemispheric functioning among Japanese. In a series of experiments Tsunoda found what he felt were marked differences between Japanese and people of other nationalities (even Chinese and Koreans) in their left- and right-brain functioning. Some of his followers have gone so far as to claim that the uniqueness of the Japanese brain is to blame for inadequate English language mastery by the Japanese! At the same time, Edwards and others contend that most Westerners are too left-brained: too analytical, too systematic, too structured.

---

[5]E. Paul Torrance, *Your Style of Learning and Thinking* (Bensenville, IL: Scholastic Testing Service, Inc., 1987).

[6]Betty Edwards, *Drawing on the Right Side of the Brain* (Los Angeles: J.P. Tarcher, 1979).

[7]Tadanobu Tsunoda, *The Japanese Brain* (Tokyo: Daishukan Shoten, 1978). [in Japanese]

While there may be many differences between left- and right-brain characteristics, it's important to remember that the left and right hemispheres operate together as a team. Messages are sent back and forth such that both hemispheres are involved in the activity inside the human brain. Most learning contexts involve the capacities of both hemispheres, and often the best solutions to problems are those in which each hemisphere has participated optimally.

Nevertheless, we all tend to have one hemisphere that is more *dominant*. As is the case with the learning styles already discussed, you probably favor one side of your brain or the other. As you can see in the chart above, left- and right-brain differences in fact capture some of the characteristics of those learning styles. Other left/right contrasts may highlight some new factors that could affect your language learning process.

According to some research studies, people learning foreign languages in natural environments (that is, not in the classroom) appear to do more right-brain processing in the early stages than in the more advanced stages of learning. So, our natural tendency may be to absorb language at the outset, and to do more analytical focusing only at later stages of development. Most of our foreign language classes do just the opposite: they teach all the nuts and bolts at the beginning. Only much later in the process are students expected to get a "feel" for the language.

Alex was an exception. In his case, early left-brained efforts worked to his advantage, but most of us won't do well if our left brain dominates too much.

In your foreign language learning experience, you are likely to favor your left brain by overanalyzing and by focusing too much on the details instead of backing off and allowing some of your intuition, spontaneity, and synthesizing capacities to take over. Your efforts would be better directed at getting into your "right mind." Beyond that, of course, it's important to stay as balanced as possible in your approach. Use both of those hemispheres in that all-important teamwork.

Exercises for Week Nine

1. In this test,[8] each item has two contrasting statements. Between the two statements is a scale of five points on which you are to indicate your perception of which statement best describes you. Boxes 1 and 5 indicate that a statement is very much like you; boxes 2 and 4 indicate that one statement is somewhat more like you than the other statement; box 3 indicates no particular leaning one way or the other.

---

[8]Adapted from E. Paul Torrance, *Your Style of Learning and Thinking* (Bensenville, IL: Scholastic Testing Service, Inc., 1987). Permission granted by Scholastic Testing Service.

Example:

I prefer speaking to large audiences.	1	2	3	4	5	I prefer speaking in small group situations.
	☐	☐	☐	☒	☐	

Box number 4 has been checked to indicate a moderate preference for speaking in small group situations.

	1	2	3	4	5	
1. I remember names.	☐	☐	☐	☐	☐	1. I remember faces.
2. I respond better to verbal instructions.	☐	☐	☐	☐	☐	2. I respond better to demonstrated, illustrated, symbolic instructions.
3. I am intuitive.	☐	☐	☐	☐	☐	3. I am intellectual.
4. I experiment randomly and with little restraint.	☐	☐	☐	☐	☐	4. I experiment systematically and with control.
5. I prefer solving a problem by breaking it down into parts, then approaching the problem sequentially, using logic.	☐	☐	☐	☐	☐	5. I prefer solving a problem by looking at the whole, the configurations, then approaching the problem through patterns using hunches.
6. I make objective judgments, extrinsic to person.	☐	☐	☐	☐	☐	6. I make subjective judgments, intrinsic to person.
7. I am fluid and spontaneous.	☐	☐	☐	☐	☐	7. I am planned and structured.
8. I prefer established, certain information.	☐	☐	☐	☐	☐	8. I prefer elusive, uncertain information.

Scale: 1 2 3 4 5

#	Left statement	1	2	3	4	5	Right statement	#
9.	I am a synthesizing reader.	☐	☐	☐	☐	☐	I am an analytical reader.	9.
10.	I rely primarily on language in thinking and remembering.	☐	☐	☐	☐	☐	I rely primarily on images in thinking and remembering.	10.
11.	I prefer talking and writing.	☐	☐	☐	☐	☐	I prefer drawing and manipulating objects.	11.
12.	I get easily distracted trying to read a book in noisy or crowded places.	☐	☐	☐	☐	☐	I can easily concentrate on reading a book in noisy or crowded places.	12.
13.	I prefer work and/or studies that are open-ended.	☐	☐	☐	☐	☐	I prefer work and/or studies that are carefully planned.	13.
14.	I prefer hierarchical (ranked) authority structures.	☐	☐	☐	☐	☐	I prefer collegial (participative) authority structures.	14.
15.	I control my feelings.	☐	☐	☐	☐	☐	I am more free with my feelings.	15.
16.	I respond best to kinetic stimuli (movement, action).	☐	☐	☐	☐	☐	I respond best to auditory, visual stimuli.	16.
17.	I am good at interpreting body language.	☐	☐	☐	☐	☐	I am good at paying attention to people's exact words.	17.
18.	I frequently use metaphors and analogies.	☐	☐	☐	☐	☐	I rarely use metaphors or analogies.	18.
19.	I favor logical problem solving.	☐	☐	☐	☐	☐	I favor intuitive problem solving.	19.
20.	I prefer multiple-choice tests.	☐	☐	☐	☐	☐	I prefer open-ended questions.	20.

Scoring directions.

Score each item as follows: Some of the items are scored according to the numbers at the top of each column of boxes, others are *reversed*. For the following items use the indicated numbers on the test page:

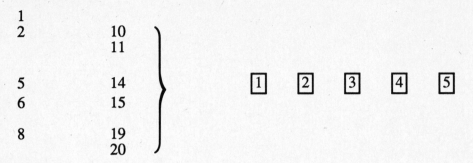

1
2   10
       11

5   14
6   15

8   19
       20

The rest of the items are *reversed* in their scoring. Score the following items using the numbers indicated at right.

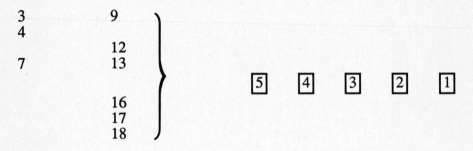

3   9
4
       12
7   13

       16
       17
       18

Now total up all scores: _____

    This was a test of left- and right-brain preference. A score of sixty is the mid-point. The scoring chart below indicates that a score of sixty plus or minus three is a toss-up:

Above 70	Quite right-brain oriented
64-70	Moderately right-brain oriented
57-63	No particular dominance on either side
50-56	Moderately left-brain oriented
Below 50	Quite left-brain oriented

    Does the score seem to fit your own view of yourself? If not, go with your intuition, since tests like these aren't accurate for everyone. However you line up on left- and right-brain differences, capitalize on the strengths of your own orientation. Be aware of those strengths and don't let yourself rely too much on one type of functioning. If you scored close to the midpoint, that may be a rather good indication of your ability to function with both sides of the brain.
    Now continue reading the chapter where you left off; it will help you interpret your score.

2. In your journal, react to the list of left- and right-brain differences. Is it possible that the insights you've gotten might lead to your doing something differently in the classroom? Or on your own, as you do homework or practice the language?

3. Share your left-/right-brain profile with classmates or your conversation group. Talk about your differences. Can you see how both left- and right-brain processing are important in order to successfully learn a foreign language?

CHAPTER TEN

Superlearning

Have you ever seen one of those advertisements that promises you super powers to learn tremendous numbers of facts in a very short period of time? You're told that you can assimilate material several times faster than you do now. That your brain is an untapped resource. And that you can learn all these things without stress.

Wouldn't you love to be able to put such power to work on your foreign language? Right now you're in the heaviest part of your course, with final exams just four or five weeks away. This would be a perfect time for you to assume some magical ability to put all this stuff perfectly in place.

Well, there's good news and bad news. The good news is that you may *not* be tapping your full potential and that there are indeed some things you might try that could help you to internalize greater quantities of material. The bad news is that there's no magic that you can work. No one can give you a quick set of instant recipes that will do the job for you effortlessly. Let's concentrate on the good news for now.

IQ and language learning The first piece of good news is that a high IQ, as it's traditionally measured, isn't essential for successful foreign language learning. People with average intelligence can be very adept at learning a language, and those with exceptionally high IQs can be miserable failures.

The reason for this apparent contradiction is that IQ tests measure very specific verbal, mathematical, and logical abilities, while language learning requires much more than these abilities. Language learning requires other forms of intelligence, such as:

- interpersonal communication ability (for perceiving and understanding other people)
- self-knowledge (for developing your own unique pathway to success)
- musical ability (for hearing the intonation and rhythm of the language)
- muscular coordination (for pronouncing the language)

All of these abilities are forms of intelligence that aren't calculated into IQ tests.

So if you feel you don't have an exceptionally high IQ, or if you tend not to shine brightly in standardized, multiple choice tests, take heart! You most likely have other abilities that are probably even more important for language learning. If, on the other hand, you're among those who do well on IQ tests, you can make use of those verbal, logical, and mathematical abilities for taking in great quantities of information, but you may have to put in some extra effort to *use* that information for communication in real-life situations.

Supermemory The second bit of good news is that you really can reach down a bit deeper into the capacities of your mind and improve memory, especially for vocabulary, which is almost always something the foreign language learner struggles to remember.

Consider the following story:[9]

A man walks briskly to the back of the auditorium filled with nuclear scientists, some of them Russia's most brilliant. Mikhail Keuni, an artist, tells a volunteer on the stage: "Turn that big blackboard around so that it's facing away from me. Take a piece of chalk and cover the blackboard with circles. They can intersect. They can be inside one another. Draw them any way you wish." The volunteer madly draws dozens of circles. As the board is spun around for Keuni to glance at it, the audience laughs. It's white with circles. Keuni's eyes scarcely blink. In two seconds he calls out the total: "167!" Five minutes of careful calculation by the audience then verifies Keuni's answer.

Reportedly, Keuni was similarly able to channel his extraordinary abilities toward second language learning. When his tour plans called for a trip to Japan, he is said to have become completely fluent in Japanese in one month. Later a trip to Finland prompted him to master Finnish in a week!

What accounts for such incredible mental powers? Do people like Keuni have a unique, innate set of capacities? Can ordinary people like us avail ourselves of what we might think of as superhuman abilities? The experts say that we only use a small fraction of our brain capacity. Is there some way to release a significantly greater fraction?

These questions might be answered in the light of what has been called *superlearning* or *speed learning*, that is, various techniques for getting lots of things into your brain in a short time.

According to Bulgarian psychologist Georgi Lozanov,[10] superlearning power is a natural human ability, available to anyone who will work hard enough to achieve it. Through his method of *Suggestology*, students are put into relaxed states of consciousness, with quiet music playing in the background. Then they are given large quantities of various forms of subject matter: math, physics, history, foreign language. Lozanov's experiments claim phenomenal results: in 1977 one study concluded that foreign language students had absorbed as many as 3,000 words a day in Suggestology classes!

Suggestology capitalizes on the principle that the brain is most receptive in that pre-sleep phase during which pulse and blood pressure decrease and certain brain waves are slightly altered. In *relaxed concentration*, we are restfully alert, and able to take in large masses of data that we otherwise block out.

The suggestology method isn't isolated. You don't have to look very far in a bookstore these days to find a whole rack full of tapes that claim to do wonders for your stress level, remove fears of various kinds, and teach you new skills. A Japanese educator named Suzuki is well known

---

[9]Sheila Ostrander and Lynn Schroeder, *Superlearning* (New York: Dell Publishing Company, 1979), p. 13.

[10]Georgi Lozanov, *Suggestology and Outlines of Suggestopedy* (New York: Gordon and Breach Science Publishers, 1979).

for his "sleep teaching" methods of teaching kids to play a musical instrument. Students go to sleep at night listening to tapes of the music they're learning to play. The next morning they can play their pieces with more ease.

Keep in mind, though, that sleep teaching is a bit of a misnomer. The key is to take in the material just *prior* to going to sleep, when conditions are optimal, and before you lapse into unconsciousness.

You also do yourself a favor if you take some of the claims for supermemory with a grain of salt. What many of the experiments don't tell you is what *else* you have to do to achieve outstanding results in your quest for foreign language fluency. Even the extensive Suggestology experiments in Bulgaria included a great deal of other work accompanying the "concert" sessions (during which taped music accompanied language spoken by the teacher): exercises, role plays, written work, and conversation practice. So, don't get all your hopes up that some pre-sleep tapes are going to work a miracle for you. You have to work hard at using the language you're learning in as many real-life situations as you can. You've got to see to it that you aren't just parroting a bunch of stuff from tapes.

But is there a ray of hope that you might improve your learning of this foreign language by sitting in a comfortable chair, relaxing, and listening to tapes of people pronouncing words and engaging in conversations? To some extent, there is. Through such a technique, you might be able to get some important input that will later become a part of your conscious storehouse of knowledge in the language. Suggestology sessions with do-it-yourself home-study tapes might help you. By all means, don't rule out the possibility just because it sounds a little bizarre.

Exercises for Week Ten

1 . It's worth a try for you to get some foreign language tapes (language lab tapes or tourist survival tapes, for example) and try some adaptation of Suggestology on your own. Find some soothing music to play on one tape player, record player, radio, or compact disk player. Classical music or new age music will probably work well. On another tape recorder, set up your language tape. Assume a meditative, comfortable position where you won't go to sleep but you can relax your body. (Sitting in a comfortable chair in an upright position should work.) Start the music and just relax for about five minutes, breathing slowly and deeply and setting your mind in neutral. When you feel quite relaxed, start the foreign language tape. (Make sure the music isn't too loud or too soft in comparison.) Just listen to the tape; don't try to respond or repeat anything. Go all the way through the tape at least once. Repeat this sort of session several times.

2 . In your journal, record your reactions to doing Exercise 1. How did you feel? Were you too consciously aware of the experiment you were going through? Did you really relax and just let the words and the music both come into your consciousness? Within the next few days of doing those sessions, do you notice any difference in your retention or fluency?

3 . To tap some of your own mental resources, try out the following strategies for vocabulary retention, if you haven't already done so:

- use rhyming and sound-alike words to remember vocabulary
- make lists of words and do word grouping
- use flash cards
- use phonetic symbols to write words down
- make up sentences that use words you want to remember
- repeat those sentences to yourself or with a partner

Don't sell yourself short! You can no doubt take in a lot more information if you just make up your mind that you can do it and then exert some effort!

4 . How high do you think your IQ is? Look at the four other forms of intelligence that are important for language learning, and ask yourself how good you are at those forms:

- interpersonal communication ability (for perceiving and understanding other people)
- self-knowledge (for developing your own unique pathways to success)
- musical ability (for hearing the intonation and rhythm of the language)
- muscular coordination (for pronouncing the language)

CHAPTER ELEVEN

Untie the Apron Strings of Your Mother Tongue

In Mark Twain's *The Innocents Abroad*,[11] a French-speaking guide introduces himself: "If ze zhentlemans will to me make ze grande honneur to me rattain in hees serveece, I shall show to heem everysing zat is magnifique to look upon in ze beautiful Paree. I speaky ze Angleesh parfaitmaw."

Can't you just hear the young French entrepreneur in his French accent? We're all quite good at recognizing accents. Who wouldn't be able to identify a strong German accent? Or Italian? Or Latin American? Or Japanese? We can easily identify these accents because their particular sound systems and grammatical patterns contrast with those of English. The sound systems, especially, are usually dead giveaways.

Think about your language and the particular sounds that are hard for you. Most likely, they're hard because they don't exist in English. So, if you're learning:

- French, you'll probably have some problems with the French /r/, the vowel /u/ (as in *tu*), and some other vowels.
- German, you could encounter problems with the /r/ sound, the /ch/ (as in *machen*), the umlaut /ö/ (as in *mögen*), and others.
- Spanish or Italian, the /r/ again may cause a little difficulty, along with stress and intonation patterns.

You, too, are probably easily identifiable as an American when you speak your foreign language since very, very few of us ever attain absolutely perfect accents. And not many of us get to the point in a language where we have such a comprehensive grasp of grammatical patterns that we can pass as a native speaker in that respect, either. So we're pretty well stuck with this native language system that we automatically use as a reference system, or map, for the foreign language.

Why does our mother tongue get in the way? Well, anytime you learn something new, you draw on a backlog of experiences and knowledge that you hope will help you. If you're just learning to ski, for example, you'll bring to that new experience a number of skills previously learned: walking, running, sliding down a hill, balancing on a railroad track, roller skating, skateboarding, ice skating, sledding, and so on. On a pair of skis, as you try to keep your balance, make turns, control your speed, and, most importantly, come to a stop, you *transfer* your previous experiences to the present one.

---

[11]Mark Twain, *The Innocents Abroad*, vol. 1 (New York: Harper and Brothers, 1869), p. 111.

In learning a foreign language, you also transfer. In this case your native language is the previous skill that you transfer. Since it's the primary set of previous skills that you have to rely on, you're inclined to *map* the new skills onto the old, tried and true ones.

How important is this mother-tongue interference? And is there anything significant that you can do about it?

First of all, there's something you need to accept about your foreign language learning process: unless you started learning this language before the age of puberty (usually around 11-13 years old), the chances are slim that you'll develop a perfect accent. Perfect, here, means sounding exactly like a native in the foreign language. So your best bet right now is to work hard at the sounds of this language. Don't settle for anything less than you are capable of in pronouncing the language. Get to the point that you are "credible." But don't tear your hair out if your teacher or native speakers say that you sound like an American!

Don't forget that your American accent can in some ways be looked at as part of your own uniqueness. Where would Russian comedian Yakov Smirnoff be today if he spoke with a perfect American accent? Or actors like Ricardo Montalban? Our accents can be part of the charm that we carry with us.

The positive element in your pathway to success is that you can indeed to a long way toward acquiring a good, if not a very good accent in the foreign language, and that should be your goal. With a good to very good accent, you can communicate clearly and avoid being misunderstood. And clear communication is, after all, the ultimate goal in language learning. Later on, you can worry, if it's all that important, about whether you could pass as a native. But now, that shouldn't be your concern. It's much more important to work toward feeling comfortable and fluent in the language than it is to break your back trying to sound perfect.

Is there something you can do to attain a very good accent in the foreign language? Yes! The first step, which you have probably already taken by now, is to talk without worrying about what you sound like. You may feel very foolish and your classmates may laugh. Let them laugh; just laugh at yourself with them.

Then, as your inhibitions diminish, start listening to yourself carefully. Whenever you speak, notice the sounds of the language, the rhythm and stress patterns—the "flow" of the language. You can help yourself along by doing a lot of listening where you specifically do *not* try to get the meaning of the language; rather, you listen just for the sounds. Pick up on certain sounds or sound patterns, and then just keep repeating them to yourself.

Now, what about the rest of this language: the grammatical patterns, the verb system, the word order, the prepositions, articles, words, idioms, and all the rest? Here, too, your native tongue keeps getting in the way. All your life you've been in a groove—English—and now you find it hard to get out of this groove and into other ways of saying things. How do you throw off these comfortable ways of thinking?

One of the first rules of foreign language learning is to avoid constant translating to or from your native language. We tend to think of a word or phrase in English first, then translate it into the foreign language. We're always banking on the native language to bail us out in some way. What you have to try to do is to think directly in your foreign language.

Don't always insist on an English equivalent for words or phrases. Just accept them for their meaning and purpose in the foreign language. Untie the apron strings of the native language!

Ultimately it's impossible to avoid some reference to English as you move along. Don't fret. English will always be your native language and will always be more comfortable for you. In some ways, you'll find that this native language of yours actually *helps* you, especially if your foreign language is in the same general family of languages, like German, French, Spanish, or Italian. These languages have many things in common: cognates, certain grammatical patterns, a number of vowel and consonant sounds, etc. Those are things you don't have to learn afresh.

Children can teach you a lesson on how to go about learning a foreign language. They tend to move directly into a foreign language. They don't worry about what the native language equivalents are. They don't mentally translate things as they're listening or speaking. Your best bet would be to try being a little more childlike.

Exercises for Week Eleven

1. If your university has a language lab, do this exercise there. If not, then, in the privacy of your own room, get tapes in the foreign language (tourist survival tapes might do), and do lots of listening and repeating, listening and repeating. The language lab should be set up so that you can record your own voice. If you don't have a lab, find a second tape recorder, record yourself as you repeat sentences, then listen to yourself. How do you sound? Try to identify what you're doing that isn't quite right, and then keep repeating sentences. Don't be afraid to just try saying things, no matter how hard it seems.

2. You might be ready now to see a movie *without* subtitles. That will force you to deal directly with the language. Try to see something that your teacher would recommend for its simplicity, because movies are not easy to follow unless you have a good command of the language.

3. Pick up some simple prose in the foreign language—a short story, a very simple reader, or whatever. Try reading it without a dictionary and somewhat rapidly. If you see words you don't know, just read on and try to infer meaning from the rest of the passage. Whatever you do, don't translate the passage, in your mind, into English. The first time you read this way, it may seem awkward. That's okay. Stick with it for several weeks, and you should gradually find that you're taking in more than you thought you could.

4. From your teacher, your textbook, or some other reference, find out what the most common errors are that English speakers make in learning your foreign language. In your journal, make a list of the sound system errors and the grammatical system errors that are the most prevalent. Which ones do you find tough to overcome? Pick a couple of sound system problems and a couple of grammar problems and see if you can focus on those this week as you use the language. Be conscious of your own error patterns and see if you can hear yourself when you make an error. Then, try to get to the point where you can actually correct yourself.

Continue, in the weeks ahead, to focus on a couple of specific problem areas each week.

5. Don't try to be perfect! Set some acceptable goals for yourself that are challenging but not unreasonable. Write down those goals in your journal; then check back at the end of the semester and see how far you progressed.

CHAPTER TWELVE

Make Your Mistakes Work for You

> One does not learn by making mistakes, but rather by giving the right response.
>
> --Nelson Brooks, 1961[12]

We've been conditioned through almost all our schooling to think that mistakes are "bad." Errors have come to signify some degree of falling short of goals, if not outright failure. Perfection is thought to be defined as errorlessness. Some foreign language teaching methods of the 1950s and 60s unfortunately held that avoidance of errors was to be admired and sought after. The quote above by Nelson Brooks is a reflection of those beliefs.

Research now shows just the opposite to be true. Think about how young kids learn a foreign language: they make mistakes all the time. Mistakes are a natural, normal, and even necessary aspect of learning a foreign language. You can no more learn a language without making mistakes than you can learn to play tennis without ever hitting the ball into the net.

Mistakes are often the only way you can get feedback from other people on your linguistic progress. When you make a mistake in speaking the second language, you usually get some sort of response: a quizzical look, a question, a correction. That lets you know there was something in your language that wasn't quite right.

Your language slip-ups can also be the source of wonderful, tension-relieving humor. If you can develop within yourself that special ability to laugh at your own mistakes, you'll go a long way toward success.

Just how can you turn your mistakes into something good that will lead you to further success?

First of all, you need to distinguish between two important kinds of errors. You may be tempted to think that a mistake is a mistake—that any way you look at it, if people agree it's wrong, that's that. But there's an important distinction that can help you, a distinction that will free you to look at your errors more creatively and in a less cut-and-dried manner.

Some errors are simply *goofs*, and others are honest-to-goodness *mistakes*. Goofs are the little errors that anyone can make, even in their native language, that don't consistently repeat themselves. They occur at random, here and there, not because you don't know the system already, but because it's so easy to make a slip of the tongue or pen.

---

[12]Nelson Brooks, *Teacher's Manual* (New York: Modern Language Materials Development Center, 1961), p. 47.

The following sentences were produced by students of English as a foreign language (examples here are from your native language so that you can see the error without an explanation):

"The teacher was so good that the students were nailed to his lips."
"He passed out with flying colors."
"The temple elephants are paraded, and crackers burst throughout the night."

In each of these three delightful examples, the speakers were able to understand their errors immediately when they were pointed out by the teacher. Goofs, when they are called to our attention, are obvious to us and correctable. Mistakes, by definition, are not.

You can also imagine that the speakers and the rest of the class had a good laugh, especially at the first goof.

In contrast, another learner of English wrote:

"In these lakes many kinds of famous fishes are living. These fishes are serving in the restaurants near by the lakes."

Of course, it's fun to imagine fishy waiters in a restaurant! But the writer wasn't able to discern that she had made an error in this instance, even when it was pointed out to her. The particular grammatical construction involved was simply beyond her competence at the time. This, then, was a mistake.

The importance of the distinction between goofs and mistakes is that you can learn to listen to yourself and profit from that self-monitoring process. When you goof, you should be able to hear the goof and then to backtrack and try again. Mistakes, on the other hand, arise out of your deepest level of competence. They actually reveal quite accurately the system that's inside your head. They act as windows to your own conception of how the language works.

When you make a mistake, you may not yet be aware that an error has occurred; mistakes are quite possibly your very best conscious attempt to produce language, and they are a product of rules (many of them are subconscious) that have been building in your head. It takes time for your system of rules to develop within you, and you need to be patient with this process. When you do finally become aware that a rule in your head doesn't fit or is incorrect, you have to be willing to throw that rule out and revamp your system.

So, how do you detect these mistakes that may be somewhat hidden from your view? By *feedback*. Let others be your detectives. Your teacher is your greatest ally here. Listen to the feedback your teacher gives you. When you receive anything from an outright correction to a raised eyebrow, take note! Don't let that moment escape you. Try to remember right then and there what it was you said (or wrote), and see if you can figure out what you did wrong and how to correct it.

You can also profit from the feedback that others give you—classmates and anyone else you're trying to talk with. Be fully aware. Watch for the cues that something you're doing isn't quite right; then figure out where your error came from.

There are four major sources of mistakes: (1) the native language; (2) the foreign language; (3) your primary context of learning, in this case, the classroom; and (4) your own learning strategies.

The native language In the last chapter we discussed this source, and some exercises were suggested to help you begin the process of dealing with mistakes that stem from your native language.

The foreign language Quite a few of our mistakes arise from the foreign language itself. They're a product of the complexity of that particular language. If you're learning French you might at some point be tempted to say "J'ai arrivé à la gare." In this case you assumed that the verb *arriver* acts like most other verbs and takes the *avoir* auxiliary.

If you were learning English as a foreign language, you might say things like "She writed the letter," or "Does John can sing?" In both cases you made a generalization within the language that was too broad; you didn't make a distinction where one was needed.

If you can identify the source of your errors as the foreign language itself, it's actually a good sign. It indicates that you're thinking within the second language, that you're making assumptions about how that language works from the vantage point of one who already knows something about its system. Such errors are typical of the intermediate stages of foreign language learning.

Context of learning A third broad source of errors is the context within which you're learning a language and all the interpersonal and individual variables that belong to that context. Right now the classroom is your primary context. In that context, here are just some of the possible sources of error:

- The method of presentation or sequence of presentation may cause confusion. You may, for example, learn two words or patterns in the same lesson and for many weeks or months later have difficulty remembering which is which.
- The textbook you use might give some explanations that are confusing to you and thus mislead you into making a mistake.
- Other students in the class can sometimes reinforce your mistakes if they are left uncorrected.
- You might end up learning a formal or bookish way of saying something in your foreign language that leads to a mistake in a conversational setting.
- The teacher's own limitations (if any) in the foreign language could lead you to make some mistakes.

Learning strategies A fourth source of mistakes is a long list of possible strategies that you as a learner use in the process of trying to make the language your own. A typical ploy of the new language learner—one that has been advocated here—is to memorize common expressions for daily living ("How much does this cost?" "Where is the toilet?", etc.). Memorizing such phrases is a likely source of mistakes, since you're not aware of the exact meaning of what you're just learned, nor are you sure about all the appropriate contexts in which you can use something.

One of my American colleagues tells the story of a time in Japan when she was dining with some friends at a restaurant. She wanted to compliment the waiter on the food and asked one of her companions for the word for "great." Her friend gave her the word *oishi*, which actually means "delicious" and applies to food. Later in the evening at a nightclub, when an attractive young man finished a wonderful performance of a romantic song, she yelled out to him above the din of the audience, "Oishi!" That brought the house down.

There are, of course, other strategies that you might use in your second language learning experience that can end up working against you, as it were: paraphrasing to get around a difficult construction, translating or borrowing, using mime or nonverbal signals, appealing for assistance from someone else, using a bilingual dictionary, among others.

On the other hand, the fact that certain strategies may cause you to goof or make a mistake is no reason to avoid using them. A few mistakes are risks well worth taking.

Any way you look at it, you need to try to listen to yourself and to the feedback that your teacher and others provide. Occasionally, zoom in on where you're going wrong, and take some small steps to slowly eliminate errors. You may need to work on errors one by one, category by category. Maybe one week you'll work on articles; the next, verb tenses; and so on. As long as you don't get too hung up on the fact that you're making errors (remember, errors are just fine), you can listen to yourself and make your errors work for you rather than against you.

Exercises for Week Twelve

1. Set up a situation where you're trying to carry on a simple conversation with someone else. Tape record the conversation. Then play it back. Get your teacher, an advanced student, or someone else to point out your mistakes (unless you can spot them yourself). Make a list of those mistakes. Do you see any pattern? If so, this could give you a clue on what to work on.

2. Write a letter or a simple narrative in your foreign language. Don't monitor your writing. Just write as fluently as you can without a lot of attention to getting it just right. Then, look back at what you wrote. Are you able to correct yourself? To express something more accurately or appropriately? Your mistakes in the first version might give you an idea about which grammatical problems to work on.

3. Listen for the mistakes of some of your classmates. Write them down. Do you know why they made those mistakes? Paying attention to their mistakes may help you to avoid making them yourself.

4. In your journal, record your feelings about making mistakes in the classroom, where everyone is focused on you and the teacher is listening carefully. Do you just cringe at the thought of making an error? Or do you usually feel okay about it? If you feel a sense of fear and embarrassment, how do you think you can get to the point where you would be willing to take more risks? Can you keep telling yourself that it doesn't matter?

5 . Try to laugh *with* your classmates when they say funny things, and also laugh with yourself. See if you can develop the ability to make errors without feeling stigmatized. Maybe even consider yourself a bit of a comedian; it might help to ward off those feelings that you're being demeaned if you get corrected.

CHAPTER THIRTEEN

Joining the Language "Club"

The next time you're at a party with your friends, listen to people talking to each other. How often do you hear a slang word, a phrase, an expression, or a metaphor that you would never hear your parents or grandparents say? Make some mental notes of the "in-group" talk that you hear, and think about the purpose this language fulfills.

A person's spoken language is a very powerful "membership card" in what has been referred to by one researcher[13] as the "spoken language club." Think about what most clubs are like. There's an air of exclusivity about them. Those who belong and those who don't are clearly defined. Often those who are "in" have ways of seeing to it that those who are "out" are kept out; dress, money, work and even personality are usually important. There are also conventional forms of maintaining your membership. You have to follow the rules, written and unwritten, of a club in order to maintain your status. Sometimes the unwritten, covert rules are more important than the outward, formal rules. Whatever the outward form of rules, you bind yourself to the other club members by keeping those rules, and there arises a feeling of solidarity and belonging.

Think again about your friends talking with each other at the party. They're speaking a language that defines and identifies them as members of a club—a spoken language club with a lot of unwritten rules.

On my first visit to Japan I was amused by the use of English words on T-shirts, notebooks, and other personal items. Most of these words had no intrinsic meaning. They were simply emblems identified as English. A whole line of school supplies carries the label "Hello Kitty." The school kids love it. I asked one university student, who was wearing a sweatshirt with "The Nature University" printed on it, where that university was. "Oh," she answered with a little titter, "is just words, no such place exist."

In Japan, English words symbolize a club of sorts: the club of those who know—or think they know, or even who would *like* to know—English. That's an important club to belong to. Even though English is a required subject through six years of secondary school, only a tiny fraction of high school graduates in Japan actually learn to *communicate* in English. Even those who major in English in college find the goal of actually speaking English, as well as writing English, impossible to attain. So English symbolizes an intellectual status of sorts, a club to which few can belong. If you wear a T-shirt or carry a pencil case with English words on them, you gain the appearance of belonging to an exclusive club.

As you become proficient in your foreign language, you gain merit points that can ultimately admit you to the group of speakers of that

---

[13]Frank Smith, "Joining the Spoken Language Club," lecture delivered at San Francisco State University, November 3, 1984.

language. You engage in the process of joining a language club. "Club," of course, is being used here in a figurative sense, but joining a real club (where you have opportunities to use the language) is also a highly recommended activity.

In some cases you may find that current members of this figurative club will, either intentionally or inadvertently, rule you out as a possible initiate. Sometimes those lifetime members are justified in their exclusivity. When I was in Italy a few years ago, I went from Naples to Rome by train. Determined to make my phrasebook Italian work, as I got my ticket in the Naples railroad station, I asked, in my best Italian accent, "Dov'è il treno per Roma?" The station agent replied, in perfect English, "Down that hallway, second track on your left." There was no way *I* was going to be able to join *his* Italian language club! I willingly let him join my English club.

At other times you may be the object of some prejudice on the part of the club members. You might "talk funny," you might not look quite right, or you might be too loud or too quiet. If you have a hard time picturing examples, just think of your own attitudes toward some foreigners in this country. You will need to be prepared to meet biases along the way. If your skin is thick enough, you should be able to let a few rebuffs bounce off you without permanent damage.

More optimistically, you should expect that most of your language club-joining efforts will be openly welcomed by those who are already in. Often your efforts to meet others on their turf are seen as a compliment to the other culture, language, and/or country. If you just stick with it, you will readily find those who will reward you by opening the club doors.

You are what you speak One of the worst possible things you could say to someone is, "I don't like the way you talk." People can make fun of your clothing, your hairstyle, or even your ancestry, but if they ridicule the way you talk, the hurt is biting and lasting. One of the reasons that such a comment cuts so deeply is that you can't ever really hide your speech. You can change clothes and hairstyle, and you can deceive a bit on background, but the way you talk is so deeply a part of you that it does indeed define you. Speech is the emblem of who you are.

As you were growing up, your native language was the language through which you developed yourself, viewed yourself, and conveyed yourself to other people. Your native language became, and now is, a language through which you created your identity.

As you increase your fluency in your foreign language, you tend to take on a *second* identity that's intertwined with the foreign language. You will eventually (if you don't already) feel that there's a different self that's talking and interacting in the foreign language. As a child growing up in central Africa, I had a very clear conception of myself as a different person when I was conversing and mingling with my African friends. I was not African; I could never be totally African. But the self that was interacting with Africans in Kikongo was different from the identity I perceived when I was with my parents and other Americans.

The prospect, then, of becoming fluent in a foreign language takes on a pervasive psychological nature. The self that you've grown comfortable with must suddenly be faced with an additional self. A researcher once likened this acquisition of a second identity to

concept of
2nd identity

schizophrenia! You can well imagine two *personas* within you as you become bilingual, and many foreign language learners have recounted the distinctiveness of their two selves. At times a foreign language learning experience within the culture of the foreign language can indeed produce some severe culture stress. But never fear, a foreign language learning experience won't make you a schizophrenic! You simply need to grow comfortable with the prospect that there will develop within you a second mode of thinking, feeling, and acting. Eventually you'll find that you actually think differently when you're using your foreign language. You'll experience the feeling that "you are what you speak."

Exercises for Week Thirteen

1. In your journal, do a little probing on how you feel about the way you talk in your native language. Do you like the way you talk? Think about how you use your native language (in talking or writing, or even in listening and reading) to define yourself. Who would you be without that native language?

2. Think about all the differences between the way you talk and the way, say, your parents or grandparents talk. You use words, expressions, and other slang that people a generation older than you don't understand. How would you feel if you had to talk exactly as your parents do? Would you feel a little strange? Not yourself? How would you feel if your parents started using all the "in-group" expressions that you use? Now, compare all those feelings to learning a foreign language, and record your thoughts in your journal.

a cultural ?

3. Write in your journal about feelings of a second identity, if any, that have begun to appear within you. Do you fight them? Those are actually healthy feelings and signs that you're beginning to operate *within* the foreign language; it's becoming a part of you.

4. Have you, at this stage in your language learning process, ever felt shut out of your foreign language "club," in the figurative sense? That is, do others seem to be using more of the language with more ease than you? What can you do to counteract this? How can you feel more a member of the club?

5. Join a real foreign language club, if there's one available to you. It's a great way to create situations where you're forced to use the language in meaningful situations: dinner groups, parties, field trips, etc. If your institution doesn't have a language club, how about starting one? Ask your teacher for suggestions and help.

CHAPTER FOURTEEN

Learning a Second Culture

Americans are the Vikings of the world economy, descending upon it in their jets as the Vikings once did in their *drakars*. They have money, technology, and nerve. We would be wise to get acquainted with them. . . . Greet them, but after you have been introduced once, don't shake hands, merely emit a cluck of joy—"hi!" Speak without emotion, with self-assurance, giving the impression you have a command of the subject even if you haven't. Check the collar of your jacket—nothing is uglier in the eyes of an American than dandruff. Radiate congeniality and show a good disposition—a big smile and a warm expression are essential. Learn how to play golf. . . . Don't tamper with your accent—Maurice Chevalier was well liked in America. And don't allow the slightest smell of perspiration to reach the easily offended nostrils of your American friends.

--François Lierres, French journalist[14]

Learning a foreign language always entails learning a second culture to some degree, even if you never actually set foot in the foreign country where the language is spoken. Language and culture are bound up with each other and interrelated. Culture is the set of conventions and rules for operating within the language club.

On the surface you may learn words, apply rules of grammar, practice pronunciation, and all those other necessary aspects of learning a foreign language. But beneath that surface is the ultimate purpose of learning the language: to communicate with people who use that language. People don't exist in a vacuum any more than club members exist without a club. They're a part of some framework: a family, a community, a country, a set of traditions, a storehouse of knowledge, or a way of looking at the universe. In short, every person is a part of a *culture*. And everyone uses a language to express that culture, to operate within that tradition, and to categorize that universe.

So if you're planning to carry on some sort of communication with people who speak or write a given language, you need to understand the culture out of which the language emerges. Without that understanding, you'll miss out on a lot of the delightful uniqueness of the language.

As you develop some cultural awareness in the process of learning your language, one of the temptations is to oversimplify your perceptions of the other culture. This oversimplification is so common that we have developed certain cultural stereotypes.

Think about the stereotypes that you, as an American, might have regarding people from other cultures. The British are reserved, overly polite, thrifty, and precise with language, and they drink tea at four o'clock. Italians are passionate and demonstrative, and they drink red wine with pasta. Germans are stubborn, industrious, and methodical, and they drink

---

[14]François Lierres, "How to Get Along with Americans," *Le Point* (1975).

beer every night. Orientals are reserved, wise, cunning, and inscrutable, and they, too, drink tea.

But wait a minute; put the shoe on the other foot. How do these other cultures perceive Americans? We are rich, informal if not impolite, materialistic, and too friendly, as François Lierres pointed out in the quote at the beginning of this chapter. We all drive large cars, live in the suburbs, and eat at fast food restaurants. Our political leaders like to be seen with their shirtsleeves rolled up or relaxing in jeans and tennis shoes.

Not all of this sort of stereotyping of cultures is bad. We get some of our notions from legitimate cultural characteristics, and we need to be aware of those characteristics. We need to understand that the French really *are* different from Americans in important ways—and we'd better understand those differences before we do business with them or invite them to our homes for dinner.

Stereotypes have a way of broadly defining club membership. If you're careful not to attend just to the negative stereotypes, then the positive stereotypes can help to balance the picture for you. Those positives can also help you to understand that all stereotyping arises out of our particular world view. Stereotypical traits are only seen as relative to the traits of our own culture. So, Latin Americans are perceived as loud simply because we perceive them as louder than Americans; Americans, on the other hand, are perceived as loud by Japanese. Just remember that every member of a culture doesn't conform to all the stereotypes!

Stereotyping usually implies a particular attitude on your part toward the culture. And attitudes toward a culture spill over onto your feeling about the language itself. If for some reason you have a dislike of a certain nationality, you may also have a subtle dislike of the language. Obviously, your motivation to learn that language is going to be adversely affected.

The joining of the language club is going to necessitate a conviction on your part that the members of the club are "okay." You have to feel that these people are worthy, interesting, intelligent people, worth mingling with and getting to know. If you have some negative biases about the people, you'd best leave them at the door when you enter their language club. Actually, successful language learners almost always find that whatever little biases they had at the outset are quite convincingly dispelled as they interact in the foreign language with real live people. Talking with people in their language is a great equalizer.

The key to developing positive attitudes is *empathy*, the ability to "put yourself in someone else's shoes." Empathy is reaching beyond your own self and your own perspective to grasp another person's self and perspective. Developing cultural empathy is easier said than done. Each of us is so bound up in our own cultural background and experience that reaching out for other ways to experience the world is no simple task. It's essential for successful foreign language learning that you be able to bridge the gaps, to close the distance that's there.

The empathy that you develop for the culture of the language you're learning doesn't necessarily prevent you from sustaining your own native cultural identity. Just because you understand other cultures doesn't mean you close out your membership in your native language club.

The anthropologist Margaret Mead explained how she learned languages in the field. She was very much a seat-of-the-pants learner who capitalized on a great deal of empathy. In an interview[15] she once remarked:

I am not a good mimic and I have worked now in many different cultures. I am a very poor speaker of any language, but I always know whose pig is dead, and when I work in the native society, I know what people are talking about and I treat it seriously and I respect them, and this in itself establishes a great deal more rapport, very often, than the "correct accent." I have worked with other field workers who were far, far better linguists than I, and the natives kept on saying those people couldn't speak the language, although they said *I* could! Now, if you had a recording of me it would be proof positive I couldn't, but nobody knew it!

Margaret Mead felt that rapport and shared knowledge and experience were the most important factors in learning a language. Know the people, empathize with them, try to understand them fully; the language will follow.

Exercises for Week Fourteen

1. Read avidly about the culture of language you're learning. Look at magazines, documentaries, books, travel literature, and so on. Some categories to keep in mind in which you'll probably find some differences between Americans and other cultures: recreation, geography, sports, arts, jokes and humor, religion, ethnic viewpoints, traditions and customs, doing business, meeting and greeting people, and dating and courting.

2. The next time you're with any native speakers of your foreign language, notice *nonverbal* expressions:

- facial expressions: do they do anything different from typical Americans?
- eye contact: do they look straight into your eyes as they're conversing with you?
- hand gestures: how much do they use their hands and arms, and in what way?
- distance away from you when talking: do they get too close to you? Or stay too far away?

3. If you ever get a chance to travel to a country where your foreign language is spoken, do it! But, depending on where you live, opportunities to immerse yourself in the foreign language may be in your own back yard. Many metropolitan areas have ethnic communities where good chances may be available for you to practice your language. Ask your teacher for suggestions of contexts in your area where you could use your foreign language.

---

[15]Margaret Mead, "Discussion," in *Approaches to Semiotics*, Thomas A. Sebeok, et al. (The Hague: Mouton Publishers, 1964), p. 189.

4 . Check your own stereotypes. In your journal, describe the stereotypes of the country where your foreign language is spoken; then check those impressions with someone from that country. Have that person share stereotypes of Americans. You can gain some perspective from such conversations.

5 . Ask yourself—and record this in your journal—what your basic attitude is toward the people who speak the language you're learning. How positive is it? What are some negative factors? Try to figure out ways to counteract the negative by understanding the people better or by changing your own outlook.

CHAPTER FIFTEEN

The Language Learning Game

The famous musician and conductor Leonard Bernstein[16] is also an accomplished player of the language learning game. Since he travels to many other countries in the course of his work, he has made it a practice to try to learn at least some of the language of a country he is about to visit.

Before a trip, Bernstein's strategy is to spend forty hours—an hour a day—by himself with a phrase book, primarily studying vocabulary. His aim is to master a basic vocabulary of about five hundred words. He concentrates on words that he'll need in hotels, words like *soap*, *towel*, and *bathroom* (but not words like *ceiling*, *wall*, and *floor* that so often appear in language textbooks), and words used in restaurants, like *glass*, *knife*, *wine*, and *check*. He doesn't worry about names of flowers and animals that he'll have no use for. Nor does he recommend that his own choices of what to learn are necessarily what someone else should learn. Other learners should make choices according to their own needs.

Bernstein has a particular approach to learning verbs. He learns just a few of the most common verbs, and only in their simplest form. One of these verbs is always the word for *want*. That way he can say things like *I want a single room with a bath*, *I want a menu*, and *He wants a ticket to Athens*. (Note that this strategy appears to work well for him with most European languages, but he doesn't comment on its use with other families of languages.)

After about forty hours of self-study, Bernstein hires a foreign student as a tutor and passes a couple of hours a week with the tutor in simple conversation. He doesn't spend time with the tutor on drill. He does that later on his own time. A day or two before he leaves on a trip, he spends three hours with his tutor speaking only the tutor's language. When he gets to his foreign destination, he tries to go to restaurants and hotels that are somewhat off the beaten track and away from American tourists.

Bernstein reports considerable success with this method. He uses whatever resources are available to him in order to communicate and get messages across. If words fail him, he will try other ways to get his meaning across. If, for example, he doesn't know to say "I'm finished," he will say things like "Enough," or "No more." He doesn't let his lack of knowledge of the language fluster him and just keeps trying until he has communicated. He goes with his hunches and takes risks.

By arming himself with a few strategies and by having some fun with the process, Bernstein makes a game of language learning. In his preparation he uses a systematic, left-brained approach. He has a master plan and tries to fit each language into that plan. But once he's out in the

---

[16]Leonard Bernstein, "Visit As a Friend—Learn Their Language Before You Go," *House Beautiful* 116 (1974): pp. 123-124.

arena where the game is actually played out, he allows his intuition to take over, and doesn't do a great deal of worrying about whether his system is working or not.

Bernstein's formula might not work ideally for you. You may do better with less of the "homework" and more of the business of getting out there with the natives and surviving. Or your game plan in the homework phase may differ. But you should at least try diving into the task of language learning with some confidence that you'll find your own way to succeed.

How is foreign language learning like a game? Can you actually make a game of your learning process in class?

Twenty-five years ago psychologist Eric Berne's bestseller, *Games People Play*,[17] introduced the American public to the gamelike quality of relationships and communication. Berne said there were two qualities of games that distinguish them from other daily activities: 1) their ulterior nature, and 2) an eventual "payoff." Every game, according to Berne, is basically dishonest, and its outcome has a dramatic quality. Think about ordinary "real" games like chess or football. Their ulterior nature is seen in hidden strategies: in football, for example, one strategy is to appear to be setting up for a running play while actually planning a pass play. Or in chess, you may sacrifice a knight to divert the attention of your opponent while you close in on checkmate. The payoff is the win: the thrill of victory.

Human communication games, said Berne, share the same qualities. You play sexual games of flirtation just up to the point of exposing your inner thoughts; your payoff is the return of sexual messages or, better yet, action.

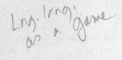

Learning a foreign language is a game, too. All the strategies that you develop to learn the language is the ulterior part. The payoff comes when you find yourself in a spot where you can actually use the language for some meaningful purpose.

It's not that hard to make your own little games of your language learning experience. When I go to a country whose language I don't know, I spend quite a bit of time with a tourist survival book learning useful phrases, à la Leonard Bernstein. During a recent trip to Yugoslavia it didn't take much effort for me to gain a fairly authentic pronunciation of a couple of dozen stock phrases. So my game was to use phrases with people in Yugoslavia and pretend I knew Serbo-Croatian. This I did, and the payoffs came when my communication goal was accomplished. I got the price of something, I ordered food and got what I asked for, I asked for directions and found places, I found bathrooms, and I thanked people profusely and endeared myself to them.

There were some unexpected payoffs. Every now and then I would have an anxiety attack when someone would start jabbering back at me in language I couldn't possibly decipher. At that point I had to find a way to graciously end the little conversation or simply say "Nisam razumio" (I don't understand) and walk away! But I did have fun and was much happier

---
[17]Eric Berne, *Games People Play* (New York: Grove Press, Inc., 1964).

playing the game than I would have been in safe enclaves of fellow American tourists, protected by translating tour guides!

You can treat your language learning process as you would a game of poker or tennis, or whatever your favorite game is. This book has dealt extensively with your ulterior game plan. Developing your own inner states of motivation and self-confidence, lowering anxieties, and becoming more of a risk taker are part of the plan. And there's clearly something ulterior about all the specific strategies you adopt to take in the words, the sentences, the rules, and so on, along with the strategies you adopt to get the language out and into the ears and eyes of others. The payoff is obvious and might even be rather dramatic. You'll surprise yourself with how much you can accomplish!

Virtually every strategy or gimmick that has been mentioned so far in this book can become a little game. And remember, games are fun. You can take a lighthearted perspective on this language learning process of yours by thinking of it as a game. So, go for the gold!

Exercises for Week Fifteen

1. Review all of the gimmicks and techniques that have been suggested in the exercises in this book, and try to view them as little games that you can play. If you've tried some before and they haven't worked, try them again, this time with the conviction that you can turn them into a game.

2. Here are some other suggestions for turning language learning into a game:

   a. The music game: Set words, phrases, and/or sentences to a familiar tune and sing them. You'd be surprised how music etches certain stretches of language into the brain. Sing these sentences back to yourself or use snatches of measures as you try to communicate.
   b. The mnemonics game: Create acronyms for conjugations or declensions. Make up phrases that associate words in your foreign language with English.
   c. The kazoo game: Focus exclusively on intonation and practice "singing" sentences through a kazoo. You'll be able to discern better the accuracy of your intonation.
   d. The noun-verb game: Try speaking a language using only nouns and verbs, and don't even worry about inflections. You'd be surprised at the payoff.
   e. The visualization game: "See" yourself speaking the language fluently, interacting with people in the second language. Then when you're actually in such a situation you will, in a sense, have "been there" before.

3. In your journal, try to write down what you think are the ten most important commandments for you to follow in successfully learning your foreign language. Try to assess yourself very candidly and honestly in terms of how you generally prefer to go about learning things; then ask yourself which styles and/or strategies are the ones that work best for you. Remember that your particular pathway to success will probably be a unique one, different from those of others in your class.

You may come up with principles like:

"I'm okay, so I can do it and do it well."
"Don't worry; don't be anxious, relax!"
"Speak up more in class and try saying things."
"Pay more attention to vocabulary."

Whatever you come up with, try to be true to *yourself*. Then, make a little poster out of your ten commandments for successful learning. Put it in a place where you'll see it often and follow those commandments!

4. Share your top ten principles with your conversation group or with a couple of others in the class. You may give one another insights into your individual pathways to success.

5. As you now move into the next semester of your foreign language (you will go on, won't you?), you might want to thumb through this book one more time. You may pick up on some things you didn't try before. As you do so, keep writing in your journal! And keep looking back through it periodically to see where you've been in this language learning journey. Best wishes!

APPENDIX

Answer to the puzzle on page 23:

The message is simply the word *fly* spelled in block capital letters. To get the puzzle, you have to look at the *white* space in between the mysterious black blotches. We are so conditioned to looking for black written symbols on white paper that our first impulse is to analyze the black blotches, which, of course, is the wrong strategy.

Often the best way to solve this puzzle is to back away from it and try to look at the whole picture with a "wide-angle lens." The word *fly* then becomes more readily apparent.

The puzzle is a good illustration of several principles of foreign language learning: (a) don't assume that all the rules of your native language will apply to the foreign language; (b) don't overanalyze the bits and pieces of the language; and (c) back off and get the general meaning, or gist, of what is said or written.

About the Author

H. Douglas Brown is Professor of English in the Master of Arts Program at San Francisco State University, and Director of the University's American Language Institute. Previously, Professor Brown taught at the University of Michigan and the University of Illinois. He was President of TESOL (Teaching English to Speakers of Other Languages) in 1980-81. From 1970-79 he was Editor of *Language Learning*, a professional journal in applied linguistics. Along with numerous articles and edited books, his textbook, *Principles of Language Learning and Teaching* (second edition, 1987), is well known in language teaching circles.